Bicycle

/

Race

BICYCLE/RACE

Transportation, Culture, & Resistance

Adonia E. Lugo PhD

Microcosm Publishing
Portland, Oregon

BICYCLE/RACE
Transportation, Culture, & Resistance

© Adonia E. Lugo, 2018

This Edition © Microcosm Publishing 2018

First published Oct 9, 2018

ISBN 978-1-62106-764-1

This is Microcosm #246

Edited by Elly Blue

Cover by Katja Gantz

Book design by Joe Biel

Distributed by PGW and Turnaround in the UK

For a catalog, write or visit:

Microcosm Publishing

2752 N Williams Ave.

Portland, OR 97227

www.microcosmpublishing.com

Library of Congress Cataloging-in-Publication Data

Names: Lugo, Adonia E., author.

Title: Bicycle, race : transportation, culture, & resistance / Adonia E.
   Lugo, Ph.D.

Description: Portland, OR : Microcosm Publishing, [2018] | Includes
   bibliographical references.

Identifiers: LCCN 2017061211 | ISBN 9781621067641 (pbk.)

Subjects: LCSH: Cycling--Social aspects--California--Los Angeles. |
   Cycling--Social aspects--Washington (D.C.) | Los Angeles (Calif.)--Race
   relations. | Washington (D.C.)--Race relations.

Classification: LCC HE5738.L67 L84 2018 | DDC 388.3/4720979494--dc23

LC record available at https://lccn.loc.gov/2017061211

MICROCOSM · PUBLISHING

Microcosm Publishing is Portland's most diversified publishing house and distributor with a focus on the colorful, authentic, and empowering. Our books and zines have put your power in your hands since 1996, equipping readers to make positive changes in their lives and in the world around them. Microcosm emphasizes skill-building, showing hidden histories, and fostering creativity through challenging conventional publishing wisdom with books and bookettes about DIY skills, food, bicycling, gender, self-care, and social justice. What was once a distro and record label was started by Joe Biel in his bedroom and has become among the oldest independent publishing houses in Portland, OR. We are a politically moderate, centrist publisher in a world that has inched to the right for the past 80 years.

Contents

CONTENTS

Part One

Transportation and Race in Southern California

Introduction

What Does Race Have To Do with Bicycling?

José Umberto Barranco was biking home from work on the sidewalk of a suburban road early one October morning in 2007 when an intoxicated young woman hopped the curb in her car and struck him.[1] I read in the local paper that he had been a busboy at a nearby Denny's for seven years. I knew the winding street he had been biking down because it leads to San Juan Capistrano, my hometown. I had walked its length many times, and passed along it in a car even more. I knew the spots where curves made it hard to keep driving at the 45 mph speed limit, even though the other drivers behind you were not slowing down.

I read about this man's death at a moment of static in my life, when Southern California's car culture was shouting over the reduce-your-carbon-footprint norms I'd adopted during my college years in Portland, Oregon. I had recently returned to Southern California to start graduate school, and my boyfriend and I had chosen Long Beach as our home base during my first year of graduate school at UC Irvine because the regular street grid and neighborhood hubs reminded us of Portland. But in my new neighborhood, drivers quickly let me know that they didn't think my bike and I belonged on the road. Legally, I was in the right; bicyclists can lawfully use travel lanes. Culturally, I was wrong; he who can travel fastest wins. What José Umberto Barranco's death said to me was that this wasn't just a matter of vehicle choice, bikes versus cars. Race

---

1 "O.C. Bicyclist Killed by Alleged Drunk Driver." *Los Angeles Times*, October 16, 2007.

and class hierarchy were mixed up in how we traveled and whose safety mattered.

Once I started trying to wrap my head around this tangle of race, place, and mobility, I realized that I'd known about it for a long time. I knew that Latinas and Latinos walked and biked around my hometown and region more than white residents did, and they were the ones who waited on corners for the infrequent OCTA bus service. I knew that the racism in south Orange County created a palpable feeling of unwelcome for immigrants, and people insulated themselves from it by getting into private cars and off exposed sidewalks as soon as they could afford to. I knew that being inside a car was the safeguard everybody was striving toward, in part because suburban sprawl made long commutes the norm. Now I noticed that most of the bicycle users I saw in Southern California had something in common with the folks walking and riding the bus: they were people of color. I later learned that black and brown men were overrepresented in bike fatalities nationwide.[2] José Umberto Barranco's death was tragic; it was also typical.

While I'd never questioned how it bled into transportation, I had been keenly aware of the racial segregation I grew up around because I didn't make sense in it. Identifying myself in the imperfect language of race and ethnicity, I'm a half-Mexican and half-white woman. My brown skin and black hair express the genes of an Indigenous people whose name I don't know, and I grew up speaking English. Not fitting on one side of race divides could be lonely, but it also let me see how flexible the world could be because some people expected the world to bend to their will while others did the bending.

---

2 See 2004 U.S. Department of Transportation study "The Pedestrian and Bicyclist Highway Safety Problem as it Relates to the Hispanic Population in the United States."

In 2007, witnessing that traveling outside of cars could be both ecologically virtuous (saving the planet, good for you!) and socially repugnant (what, you can't afford to drive?), I could see multiple sides. We'd learned long ago how harmful the shift to oil dependence had been for our planet, but people didn't want to give up their cars. In our cars we felt safe and powerful, and these feelings mattered a lot, especially for those who had to live under harsh conditions. Yet we needed to find ways to reduce our oil consumption; of that I was certain, too. I had just started planning my trajectory as a cultural anthropology doctoral student, and the conundrum of how to promote bicycling in a place dominated by the need for speed presented a potential site for turning a divided culture toward sustainability. In other words, it became my dissertation topic.

Bicycling was not the only alternative to gas-powered, single-driver travel, but the fact that it had a social movement promoting it meant that maybe there were people out there who had some thoughtful answers to my many questions. Besides the physical streetscape, what race and class systems limited our access to mobility? Who was thinking about the street safety of the people who were usually treated like a threat to public safety? Did bike commuting make someone seem unimportant, or did being an unimportant person make bicycling seem equally worthless? Why was bicycling so low-status in Southern California, when it had been a key part of Portland's appeal? Why was it normal to travel long distances between work or school and home in Southern California? What made a street safe or unsafe, and whose safety were we talking about?

What I would find through my research and through becoming a bike advocate myself was that only a few of us were asking these questions. The bicycle movement was divided over whether there was a connection between bicycling and race, because the U.S.

bike movement was itself the product of a racially segregated society. Organized networks of white people promoting bicycling in the United States had waxed and waned since the 1880s, when the bicycle had been the height of new mobility. Wealthy men and women (but mostly men) enjoyed taking over roads on two wheels so much that they lobbied for massive expansion of the public road system. When the automobile took over as king of those roads in the early twentieth century, the bicycle gradually became a vehicle for people who couldn't drive, whether due to age, poverty, or lack of access to a driver's license.

By the 1990s, the current bike movement was growing as activists of all races looked for local alternatives to exploitative global economic systems. Some participants in this iteration of the movement envisioned bicycling as a powerful tool for community resilience and grassroots action. However, I found that the dominant project was to incorporate bicycle design into market-driven urban development through lobbying elected officials and planning agencies to adopt bicycle infrastructure standards in cities across the United States. Most bicycle advocates I met were focused on increasing public spending on bicycle-oriented street infrastructure projects.

The infrastructure advocates holding this vision believed that people drove excessively and aggressively because streets were designed for driving. People would walk, bike, and use public transit if streets were designed that way, the theory went. This was what they were telling public health advocates concerned about childhood obesity and elected officials looking for ways to show their commitment to environmental quality and public safety. *If you build it, they will come* was a fundamental tenet of bike advocacy. Pay design firms to transform the built environment and eventually regular people would use it differently. This message played on repeat in most bike-related media I found, and I heard it over and over again during my eight years of ethnographic research on bicycling.

I disagree with this approach, both as an advocate for bicycling and as an anthropologist. The development-based strategy sidesteps key questions about race, place, and mobility: Who decides what to build, who gets paid to build it, and who will frolic in those future streets? If the answers point to inequity, and they very often do, so will the fruits of the strategy. My approach to changing street culture takes a step back from designing new street systems and focuses instead on the *human infrastructure* that shapes our current mobility. Culture, social networks, who we spend time with; the relational nature of being social creatures plays a fundamental role in where we live, how we travel, who we value, and, crucially, how we transition to more sustainable lifestyles. We carry our identities and histories with us as we mobilize into public spaces like streets, and from within our individual bodies we transmit norms and new ideas.

We can't design a future where race and other hierarchical structures don't matter in transportation unless we reckon with how they're embedded in today's unequal mobility landscape. When it comes to promoting bikes, I've found that the most equitable way toward sustainable transportation is through building a multiracial movement for mobility justice. Organized this way, we can join the landscape of community-based activists from many social movements who fill the intersection at the corner of ecological stewardship and undoing the inequality that has held us back from a true democracy.

I learned about human infrastructure through years of working on bike projects in Los Angeles and talking to people about bicycling in cities around the United States. I moved to Washington, D.C. in 2013 to work on racial inclusion within the organized bike movement,[3] thinking that if we wanted to build the human infrastructure to support people commuting differently, we first needed to create a social movement that reflected our country. Then I burned out, because bike advocacy already had its own technical experts and political insiders, and they weren't all invested in co-creating a multiracial agenda for their work. My passion for making bicycling into an equitable climate change solution dimmed at that point, and I spent a few years tracing painful colonial histories, both personal and place-based. This reflection gave me a new perspective on my own advocacy that I've used to craft the narrative in this book.

My decolonizing project also informs where I see us going from here. More people in the U.S. are opposed to a multiracial consensus than many white people wanted to believe prior to November 2016. Pursuing sustainability through people power is more strategic than ever. Politics is its own infrastructure, necessary because through it flows the right to spend our public resources, but it has a hierarchical culture where few of us can speak on our own terms. We need to organize ourselves in a way that connects our individual bits of privilege across a living grid, a grid that shows the links between transportation and housing, policing, and economic justice. This is what it will take to advocate for the street safety of people who face multiple insecurities at once, like José Umberto Barranco, who died on his way home from work. Our concept of "safety" must expand outward and outward until everyone has their needs met.

In order to bring our privilege and power to that safety project, each of us must understand where we come from and what we have to offer. The bike has been my vehicle for exploring what I can do as an individual even while I'm tied into systems that feel

3 You can find a longer explanation of what I mean by "organized bicycling" in the introduction to the 2016 collection *Bicycle Justice and Urban Transformation: Biking for All?* co-edited by Aaron Golub, Melody Hoffmann, Gerardo Sandoval, and me.

so hard to change, but it's not black and white. Riding a bike, I've felt strong; navigating white supremacy in bike advocacy, I've felt powerless. Like many analytical people, I'm of two minds about much of what I've seen, and this book reflects the both/and reality I inhabit. To all of you have been in dialogue with me along the way, or whose words leapt like fire from the page: thank you for ensuring I wasn't alone.

A View from the Borderlands

1

CALIFORNIA   A R I Z O N A   SANTA FE

JACUMBA
EL CENTRO
HOLTVILLE   YUMA
MEXICALI SAN DIEGO   ALBUQUERQUE   AMARILLO
YOME WELLTON
MOHAWK   N E W   M E X I C O
GILA BEND GUCKEYE   PHOENIX
FLORENCE   LORDSBURG
VAIL BENSON   DEMING LAS CRUCES ROSWELL
TUCSON TOMBSTONE   MESILLA PARK
BISBEE DOUGLAS   FT. HANCOCK
NOGALES   RODEO   SIERRA BLANCA   T E X A S
NACO AGUA PRIETA EL PASO   VAN HORN
KENT   FT. STOCKTON
M E X I C O   VALENTINE MARFA ALPINE MARATHON SANDERSON SHEFFIELD
                                        FT. DAVIS   OZONA SONORA ROOSEVELT
                                                                ROCK SPRINGS MT. HOME KERRVILLE COMFORT BOERNE SCHERTZ
                                                         DEL RIO LEON SPRINGS
                                          VILLA ACUNA UVALDE EAGLE PASS PLEASANT
US 80   PIEDRAS NEGRAS DILLEY THREE RIVERS
OST   LAREDO ALICE
                                        NUEVO LAREDO FALFURRIAS
THRU THE LANDS OF
AMERICA'S ANCIENT HISTORY
CONNECTING
FLORIDA · MEXICO · CALIFORNIA ·
NATIONAL HEADQUARTERS
SAN ANTONIO ~ ~ TEXAS   BROWNSVILLE MATAMOROS

MAP SYMBOL:
✚ OLD SPANISH MISS

In the U.S. imagination, Southern California is a still-wet canvas where seekers who make their way here can paint whatever picture they like against a backdrop of natural beauty. My California is different; I grew up feeling watched by ghosts.

Archaeological records show that people had inhabited the region for at least ten thousand years before Spain sent the Cabrillo Expedition to what they called Alta California in 1542. In 1769, the Spanish royal government decided to settle the region as a guard against English, Russian, and French territorial encroachment. They were aware of the presence of people here, which is why along with their soldiers they sent Padre Junípero Serra, a priest in the Franciscan Catholic fraternal order, to continue a chain of earlier missions that Jesuit priests had started down south in Baja California. In so doing, they fundamentally altered life for the Tongva, whose ancestral lands are what we now call Los Angeles, the Acjachemen in what is now Orange County, and other peoples spread across the soft-aired coastal hills and plains. Colonizing Spanish Alta California meant shattering the Native way of life and enslaving people as the property of mission settlements.

In 1776, Serra and the Spanish soldiers established a Catholic mission near a village of the Acjachemen people and called the settlement San Juan Capistrano. Two hundred and seven years later, I was born in a stucco apartment next to the railroad tracks there. My neighborhood was typical of the Spanish fantasy style that dominates Southern California, with red-tiled roofs and textured white walls. Our rented apartment sat on what local boosters call "the oldest residential street in California," Los Rios, where houses bear the names of some of San Juan's oldest surviving families. But I was not born in a restored adobe house, nor am I from a historic local family, though I have similarly mixed blood and a Spanish last name. I was born on the part of Los Rios Street that had been developed as a low-rise subdivision with hundreds of units in the 1970s. By the time I was born, it had become, to the chagrin of some white locals, a barrio filled with immigrant families, most of them from Mexico.

There was a wall dividing my neighborhood, the Villas, from Historic Los Rios Street, but people passed between the quaint section and the heavily policed local "ghetto" on foot. Until I left for college at age seventeen, I liked to roam around the quiet streets of the historic district, which served as the backdrop when I imagined myself into L.M. Montgomery's novels about dreamy girls like me. It was my Californian Avonlea. As a kid, I got a thrill from thinking that ghosts might drift up from Trabuco Creek, the concretized channel that bounded one side of the Los Rios district while the train tracks bounded the other. I didn't want to see *La Llorona*, the Weeping Woman, who drowned her own children to spite their faithless father, and who wanders the waterways of the Spanish-speaking world mourning her murdered babies. In San Juan, she appeared in a white dress, crossing the tracks in the night. A friend told me she woke up one night and saw a Native woman sitting on her dollhouse. It was common knowledge among us kids that this friend's subdivision, the Village, had been built on an Indian burial ground. My guess is this concept came from a horror movie like *The Shining* rather than local knowledge.

By this time we had moved to another apartment in the Villas, on Calle La Zanja. A *zanja* is a sewer ditch. Either our street covered the colonial drainage system or the developer who built the condos thought it sounded pretty. I feel weird now about how casually we rubbed against the colonial past, but it was normal to treat tragedy like some *Dukes of Hazzard* hijinks where I grew up. A certain kind of official history had an ongoing life in San Juan. In school, we celebrated Swallow's Day every March 19, when the town's tourist economy climaxed in a festival that encouraged visitors to imagine that Mission San Juan Capistrano, which has long been restored as a museum, might still attract the flocks of migrating birds it once had when it was a series of crumbling adobe arcades. On the Saturday closest to the 19th, a parade ran along Camino Capistrano through lines of sunburned spectators, and horses' hooves clacked along with the popping of cap guns.

Over at San Juan Elementary, sandwiched between the Mission and the eight lanes of the 5 freeway, principals and teachers wearing plastic sheriff's badges and boots would jokingly warn their pupils during the week before each parade that if we did not dress up like cowboys, we would be locked up in the rusting cage on Los Rios. A docent told us on a school tour that long ago a little boy had hung himself with a bootlace in that cell, ashamed of having stolen a loaf of bread. This maudlin ritual was meant to instill in us a sense of place that was itself rooted in revisionist nostalgia, a cowboy vision of a white past for our town that had more to do with Orange County's Republican present than with the history of the local tribe and Mexican California. We were little brown-eyed bundles of proof that California never really stopped being part of Latin America, but nobody pointed that out to us behind the Orange Curtain.[4]

---

4 For a great overview of Orange County history and its ambivalent relationship with immigration, check out Gustavo Arellano's book *Orange County*.

Along with others, the feminist theorist and poet Gloria Anzaldúa called the home of people like us the borderlands, referring both to the geographic zone straddling Mexico and the United States and to our marginal state of being. She used it to describe her own in-betweenness as a Chicana lesbian whose tejano Spanish did not match that spoken in Mexico. We can chafe against the borderlands or find comfort within them, but the colonial encounter, its conflicts and affinities, remains alive in our blended blood. We lack the protection that's supposed to come with living clearly on one side, safe from the real or perceived dangers of the other. The everyday work of maintaining the divide falls to the people who cross boundaries regularly, like the gardeners and the maids and the nannies and the mixed-race, straight-A students like me.

I didn't find the term "borderlands" until I was an adult, but I'd always known that the border was not a fixed line. My parents divorced when I was small. I had grown up with my white mother's family, though I more closely resembled our Mexican neighbors in San Juan, thanks to my father's DNA. We spent our weekends at Grandma and Great Grandma's beach house up the coast in Corona Del Mar and during the week we witnessed the precarity of immigrant life on our block. Some of us at San Juan Elementary and later Marco Forster Junior High were safe from the border, but others weren't. It chased families up the state.

The border didn't chase me, as the U.S.-born child of a U.S. citizen, but I saw it catch others. At the train station in San Juan one day, a train roared in from San Diego and stopped. As the *ding-ding-ding* of the crossing gates drowned out all other sound, I watched a man, woman, and child step off the train, looking downwards. Immediately they were put under arrest by Border Patrol agents who had been waiting there. I could see the family's fatigue. Who knows how long it had been since they had slept or eaten? They were the embodiment of the signs we saw on the freeway when we drove south toward San Diego, which showed the panicked outlines of a man, woman, and child dashing wildly across the endless lanes of traffic. "Caution" it said in English, warning you to watch for these criminals. "Prohibido" it said in Spanish, informing the criminals that it was illegal to run across the freeway. Kids on my school bus perfected their ability to mimic a police siren, following their lilting *oo-ooh-oop* with shouts of *la migra* out the window, aimed at other brown people walking by.

I was safe because my mother's family had been in Southern California since the 1890s, when my maternal great-grandparents Otto Meyer and Vera Everett were born in San Bernardino to settler families of European descent. My mother, Laurene, surprised her family and moved to Mexico at the end of 1969 after meeting my father there on a road trip that summer. By the time I was born in 1983, she had lived in rural Nayarit, was bilingual, and had moved the family to Orange County to be close to her mother and grandmother. My mom didn't go to college like her brother and sister but her cross-cultural life gave her a keen awareness of the racism her five half-Mexican kids experienced. She raised us to question everything and to take responsibility for our effects on the world around us. Laurene's participation in the 1980s culture of personal transformational work translated into her parenting in many ways.

If my grandma Kathryn, who lived until I was 10, or my great-grandma Vera, who lived until I was 12, ever felt judgment about their descendants' mixed heritage, they kept it to themselves. They did not share my grandfather Lawrence's vicious hatred for non-whites. He disowned my mother when she married a Mexican man. My mother never tried to minimize the inappropriateness of her father's racism, even after he "forgave" her and his second wife started sending us Christmas presents from where they lived in New York City. I only met him a few times, and for a long time I thought Grandpa was a shameful outlier. But over the years, in talking with friends who spent more time with their grandfathers, I've learned that this attitude was very normal for white men of his generation. It was my mother's choice to stand up to it that set us apart.

My mom used the term "white flight" to explain why by the time I went to college she was the only white lady in our formerly mixed neighborhood. White people didn't want to live around brown people because of racism, she said. In junior high, the town's two elementary schools came together, and I learned that I'd attended what white twelve year-olds called "the Mexican school." (Only years later did I realize that this term was a holdover from the era of legal racial segregation in Orange County schools.) I had a white friend in high school whose dad wouldn't let her sleep over at my house because of our neighborhood. This was racism, Mom said.

Laurene did her best to create a sanctuary where it was okay for me to be white and brown at the same time growing up, but she couldn't change the fact that south Orange County did not believe in people like me. A brown kid close to white relatives instead of faraway tíos, tías, and abuelos in Nayarit; part of a family that fell apart so loudly the neighbors called the cops; the top of my class and integrated with my Latino peers in elementary school; segregated into advanced classes with wealthier, whiter children once we entered junior high. I learned how to be invisible at school and in the immigrant neighborhood where I was born, but there were always reminders that I was different. Like the cop who pulled me over for running a stop sign in my car when I was seventeen, who let me go without a ticket when I said, yes, I was going to college at the end of the summer. "Good, you're getting out of here," he said approvingly. Getting out of the place where

I was born, because I was better than them. I was so mad at the world that told me this. It felt like the only thing I could do to combat the lingering horror of racism was to flee Orange County.

That's why I decided to go to college in Oregon, a place I'd only read about in Beverly Cleary's books. But boy did I feel lonely when I got there. Homesick in my dorm room, for the first time my hand stopped turning the radio dial when I landed on a hip-hop station. In the Villas, when loud bassy sounds drifted into my bedroom window from passing cars, I'd turn up my own rock en español station that broadcasted out of Tijuana or the mournful English pop that my sisters trained me to love. Now I missed the audio intrusions.

Before long, my loneliness faded. With my friends at school in Portland, I didn't feel out of place for the first time in my life. For the next six years, I forged relationships through silliness, wordplay, and subcultural interests, not racial identity. It's not that I ignored my Mexican heritage, it was just part of my private life, which is why when I went to see Café Tacvba at the Roseland in 2003, I joined the crowd of enthusiastic Latino fans by myself. I wrote an undergraduate thesis on race and space in Orange County and had applied to graduate school with the plan of researching rock music in Mexico; these topics were close to my heart. And I understood what white people in Portland were really asking me when they inquired about my unusual name; they wanted to know where to locate me on the racial spectrum they carried in their heads. But living in a mostly white city and being half white, I thought about things besides racial justice until I returned to my home state. I didn't think of myself as a woman of color. I didn't know anybody who used that kind of language.

I hadn't anticipated that being a bike commuter would renew my old sense of being an outsider in Orange County, so much so that I'd develop my doctoral project around racism in my native transportation culture. Culture, as anthropologists use the word, describes shared systems of meaning and value that shape our interactions with friends, family, and strangers. It can seem invisible to us, even as we deftly maneuver our way through social situations that leave outsiders stumped. Studying a subject using anthropology's ethnographic method means observing and talking with people for as long as it takes to feel you can trace the underlying relationships between meaning and action, to know reasonably well why people do things the way they do. It seemed like there was a lot I could learn about the transportation culture that I had navigated all those years, like I could finally put my insider/outsider status to work.

Designing a project rooted in personal experience was not unusual in anthropology by the time I was getting trained in it. Ethnographers often include ourselves in the pictures we paint since we're networked into those underlying cultural infrastructures as well. This was a big shift from the early days of cultural anthropology, when researchers worked to document a diversity of cultures they saw rapidly vanishing as a result of colonial domination. Ethnographers fanned out across the continents, recording ritual practices and languages, trying to document ways of life that had already undergone massive changes as territory after territory was roughly incorporated into global political and economic systems. But by the 1960s, the field of anthropology was more certain that culture doesn't end; it changes. Culture travels. Culture is a living part of global domination, not just a casualty of it. Culture underpins our behavior, good and bad, and figuring out how to change it is challenging, both practically and ethically. And if you're talking about culture, anthropologists agreed, you're talking about power.

In early 2008, while I was reading Michel Foucault, Max Weber, and Karl Marx for my second quarter of grad school, their analyses of power colored my observations of the social life of the street. I thought about power when I noticed that a lot of the people riding bikes traveled on the sidewalk like José Umberto Barranco had been doing when he was struck. Maybe that was a strategy for complying with the culture of contempt in our streets, the mindset where we viewed fellow travelers as inconvenient obstacles between a journey's starting and ending points. We'd push the edges of red lights and perform California rolling stops because we felt like we were competing with everyone else on the road to occupy the same space. We hated having to slow down. Honking, revving the engine, swerving around, and yelling profanities were all normal responses to traffic in Southern California. I couldn't tell if drivers were treating people outside of cars worse, or if we just had less armor to absorb the disregard that so easily turned into a violent attack, but I wasn't going to let drivers chase me off the road. I was "taking the lane," participating in the bike activist move to reclaim shared public roadways.

Unlike me, the men on the sidewalk seemed to care more about survival than feeling powerful, respecting the hierarchy of the street rather than trying to disrupt it. If the car was king, they were content to stay out of His way until they could afford cars of their own. They rode mountain bikes, cheap ones you could get at Walmart or Target. They did not hang out on Long Beach's fashionable Retro Row, where road bikes like mine could be seen parked in front of businesses or in window displays. These other riders traveled on heavily congested Anaheim Street a few blocks over. They were upholding car culture even while living on the wrong side of it.

I could understand the appeal of complying with car culture as a strategy for avoiding street contempt; I'd done it myself. At seventeen, I didn't think twice about leaving the bus behind when my mom gave me her old car. Finally I, too, had my own mobile hangout zone. I'd drive to school early to get a spot in the senior lot close to the entrance, then sit and watch the sun rise over our brown hills and play My Bloody Valentine's *Loveless* on my tape deck. When I got on the bus again, it was in another state, after I left for college in 2001. The buses in Portland came more than once an hour and carried more white people than I'd ever seen on public transit. My new friends and I would smoke weed in our cozy dorm with heated floors, then walk across the dewy gray campus to wait for the 19. Onto the warm bus, to step off again into the drizzle of downtown. Our destinations were places like the mall, because I had spending money for the first time.

Having spending money was a huge thing for me. I had always felt painfully embarrassed by our lack of wealth. For teenaged me in south Orange County, being poor was part of what made me feel out of place. I remember the first time I lied about it. It didn't come up as a problem when I was in elementary school, since we were all pretty much aware of each other's family lives as neighbors. I was away at Girl Scout summer camp, having a wonderful time at age nine. I didn't have special camping utensils with my dented, makeshift mess kit. I'd been sent with regular silverware from the kitchen at home. Another girl who I became chummy with also had regular silverware. She told me it was because her family was replacing their silverware with gold-plated utensils instead. What a strange coincidence, I said, same here! It was a silly moment of peer pressure, where I told a little white lie to fit in. And in retrospect, it seems pretty weird for a little girl to bring something like that up, so maybe this was her own lie. But the moment stuck with me. I've realized as an adult how often the world I was socialized into expects me to pretend that I am intimately familiar with the security and comfort of wealth. I'm great at pretending; I've had a lot of practice.

So it was a big deal when I turned eighteen and gained access to my inheritance from the proceeds of the sale of my grandma and great-grandma's house. Corona Del Mar had become a land of millionaires and the 1940s cottages like my family's were disappearing one at a time. Developers replaced them with gaudy palazzos and modernist rectangles that left no room for a little brick-bordered garden in front like the one my great-grandma had toiled over with pride. The family sold the house in accordance with my grandma's will and it was my portion of the proceeds that let me shop at the mall when I went to college.

I drove my high school car up the coast to college one winter break, but within a year it felt like a burden and I gave it away. Getting rid of the car was part of a larger shift away from the consumerism I'd so wanted to participate in as a teen. By this time I'd lost interest in the mall and had returned to the secondhand stores that my older sisters had trained me to trawl. The car was unnecessary for the countercultural lifestyle to which I now aspired. Stuff wasn't what made me a person, although without inheriting money from the family property I might not have had the breathing room to figure that out.

Car ditched, I went back to riding the bus with my boyfriend, listening raptly as he explained the theory of visual language in film on our way back to campus with a few obscure titles from Movie Madness on Belmont. When I went home that summer, heartbroken and alone, I drove my sister's car to work at Hollywood Video.

A year later, around my graduation, a different boyfriend announced that we were going to the Goodwill to get me a bike so I could ride around town with him. Earlier in college I'd owned a lovely old cruiser that I rode on campus, but the idea of riding off into the city had never occurred to me. My new, ten-dollar bike was red and had pegs sticking out of either side of the rear wheel's hub, I guess so a friend could ride along or for tricks. "Pegs" was kind of messed up, so within a month I'd switched to a light blue Schwinn with yellow and white detail, purchased for about a hundred dollars through Portland's robust 1980s road bike market on Craigslist. I became a bike commuter. It felt amazing to launch myself across town on my bike, like climbing a mountain and getting blasted with a symphony at the same time.

Through all of this, I didn't really notice that I'd shifted my transportation outlook so fundamentally. There were plenty of other hipsters like me riding around town, so biking to the Aalto Lounge on Belmont or to dinner on Clinton hardly seemed like much of a statement. Moving to Long Beach on the border between Orange County and L.A. in September 2007 clued me in. By the end of my first year of graduate school, I was thinking about transportation culture nonstop. Transportation culture encompasses individual travel choices, the shape of our transportation systems, and the ongoing regulatory processes that maintain and change them. My research goal became understanding how street contempt continued the legacy of racism and classism. My tools were bicycles, buses, trains, and my body.

Later I would learn that some bicycle enthusiasts care a lot about the kind of bike they ride, what it's made of, how it performs on long rides and races. I haven't cultivated a knowledge of makes and models and parts manufacturers. By the beginning of 2007, I had purchased the teal and white Panasonic from the 1980s that I was still riding ten years later. I became interested in bicycling as a research subject without thinking of it as an elite sport. I was interested in it as something unsettled, like me, and as a possible tool for liberation. My bike was a vehicle for finding shortcuts and unusual paths, nothing new for an inhabitant of the borderlands. I never became a bike mechanic because I'm not interested in fixing bikes; I'm interested in how we can use bikes to fix people problems. How the social life of the street impacts the feeling of riding matters more to me than the bike technology itself.

I knew I wanted to be an activist researcher from the beginning of my project. Climate change felt far too urgent for something as passive as simply trying to understand car culture's contempt. I needed to fight it and help others fight it, too. I thought that by putting myself out there as a bike commuter, I was promoting bicycling as a possible transportation choice, one more sustainable than driving everywhere. I wanted to change our street interactions, neutralize the aggression, so that more people could stop depending on fossil fuels to travel. I didn't stop to consider whether other people would see racial justice as relevant to bicycling. From my bike I felt positioned to fight back against the legacy of colonial racism in my native land, where the ability to move freely had been curtailed for some kinds of people since at least 1769.

The Captive
and the
Carfree

2

Bobby Gadda was the reason I started riding a bike in Portland, and when he moved with me to Long Beach in 2007, we spent our weekends exploring L.A. County's built and natural landscapes using transit and bikes. We rode through the Port of Los Angeles to a secluded beach in Palos Verdes teeming with stray cats. We took a shuttle to the Queen Mary and took selfies in front of nautical equipment. That fall, we took our bikes on the Blue Line train that runs from downtown Long Beach to downtown L.A. and attended a concert at Barnsdall Park in Los Feliz, where we ran into a high school friend of mine. She told us about a group called the Midnight Ridazz, who organized nighttime bicycle rides exploring the city. Then a grad school friend discovered that this group was holding a mobile holiday toy drive, the All-City Toy Ride. With rides starting from all over L.A. County, the groups would merge in downtown L.A. and ride to a party where they would drop off toys to be donated to needy kids.

In mid-December, we met the Long Beach ride at the appointed time and place. It was a small group, mostly men. They were white. The other riders seemed to know each other, not talking much. As I later learned was the custom for these rides, we stopped at a liquor store so that people could pick up booze for the road. Then we set off to ride the eighteen miles of bike path that connects Long Beach and Los Angeles.

There are multi-use paths along many of Southern California's concretized waterways. Growing up, I spent a lot of time walking on one of these paths that connected the subdivision where I was born with Doheny Beach, about four miles away. My fellow trail users were mostly Latinas and Latinos on foot, moms walking with kids, and men wearing backpacks. Occasionally spandex-clad and helmeted white men rode by on bicycles, traveling in groups I later learned were called pelotons. I had never ridden on the L.A. River bike path, but I'd read about would-be thieves taking advantage of the fact that limited access points created long stretches of lonely trail. That December night we passed some Latino teenagers on our ride, but encountered no threat under the occasional orange glow of scattered streetlights.

The trail ended south of downtown in the industrial city of Vernon, unfamiliar territory to me. But I started to orient myself as we approached Placita Olvera, which was the meeting point that night. At the plaza we fell in with a swirling crowd, much larger than I'd expected. Hundreds, maybe thousands of people on bicycles hooted amid flashing lights. In central L.A. there were apparently a lot of these bike people. It was a racially mixed crowd. Some people had large stereo systems attached to their bikes, filling the street with music. The ride organizers distributed spoke cards, the collectible mementos of these group rides that people jam between the spokes of their bike wheels. The cards had graphics on one side and details about the ride on the reverse.

After some time circling the gazebo where I had watched mariachi bands perform on childhood trips to L.A., the large ride continued eastward. I worried that I would lose control of my bike and wobble into someone else's handlebars in the huge crowd, but in other ways riding in a group felt much safer than riding alone. I wasn't tensed against motorists' contempt, what with the human buffer around me. Many other people seemed nonchalant about the crowd, in the know, part of this exciting scene. That group ride showed me that people on bikes could use their bodies to create temporary zones where they transformed the street. After the All-City Toy Ride, Bobby and I attended a few other group rides. We started to see some of the same people and got to know their nicknames. Some folks were using bikes to explore L.A.'s history and built environment like Bobby and I had been doing. These rides had themes and might involve visiting a number of landmarks and talking about them. Other rides were more about drinking, smoking weed, and performing daredevil tricks in traffic. It seemed like there was room for all kinds of ideas, since the Midnight Ridazz website had a community forum anyone could join to discuss rides.

Through a series of encounters like these, I started to see the outlines of a social scene that overlapped with a politically-oriented bike activist culture and social movement in Los Angeles. I later learned that Midnight Ridazz had grown through a network of friends who hung around the Bicycle Kitchen bike repair cooperative, which had grown out of the social circle of bike activists living in central L.A. neighborhoods. Immersing myself in bike-related media, I found that this bike activist culture I had stumbled upon through group rides was tied into broader social networks across the country, and its participants were largely in agreement that bicycle infrastructure was the way to improve conditions for bicycling and get more people riding for transportation. Blogs with names like Copenhagenize idolized the bike-friendly streets of European cities.

The bike movement existed because in the United States there was not a public consensus that riding a bike or investing public resources in bike infrastructure were good ideas. But over the course of my research I learned that the bike movement had less interest in organizing the public to support bicycling and more interest in convincing elected officials and public employees that bike infrastructure was a good investment. Changing the public's mind would follow from changing road design, the bike movement asserted through its advocacy strategy.

I think this strategy had developed in part as a response to how hard it could be to get the public on board. The first time I witnessed outrage over bicycle infrastructure was in early 2008, when I heard neighborhood residents protesting a proposed bike facility at a city meeting near my apartment in Long Beach. The city's engineering consultant framed the project as responding to this neighborhood's homeowners' previous request that the city reduce traffic on First Street. This plan, he said, would achieve that goal by using county funds to convert their street into a "bicycle boulevard." Bike boulevards create routes for bicycling by making it inconvenient for motorists to use neighborhood streets parallel to busy arterials, making these side streets into a haven for pedestrians and bicycle users. I had often ridden on bike boulevards in Portland, and I was pleased to hear about a proposed one in Long Beach.

However, the homeowners present that night saw things very differently. First Street runs through several Long Beach neighborhoods that transition from dense tracts of apartment buildings to a more exclusive beachfront enclave. Though it's part of Long Beach's regular street grid, it has a suburban feel and many large, well-maintained homes from the early twentieth century. Some people said their historic neighborhood would be harmed by unsightly route signage, and that they had invested "hundreds of thousands or millions" in their homes. Bike infrastructure would lower their property values, they claimed. I'd never heard this before but I later learned it was a common view.

The relationship between home values and bike infrastructure is something I'll save for later; at the time of that meeting, I was more concerned about the coded racism in the homeowners' words. Having grown up in a neighborhood that outsiders called a ghetto, I tend to notice when white people express fear of exposure to black and brown people. In their remarks, the homeowners made it clear that they did not object to *bicycling*; they objected to *who* would be riding and *where*. Like many people with the economic security to take car ownership for granted, these homeowners viewed bicycling as a recreational pastime best enjoyed away from city streets. It's common in Southern California to see people idling along sidewalks and oceanfront boardwalks on bulky beach cruisers. It's also common for recreational cyclists to drive their bikes to mountain trails or other off-street destinations. Though none of the First Street homeowners said it explicitly, bicycling for *transportation* was a suspicious activity and not something the city should support in their neighborhood.

I'm guessing they'd seen the same bike users I had on busier streets, and those African-American and Latino men riding rusty bikes to get around on the cheap did not fit their vision for First Street. One elderly white woman said she biked with friends regularly, and that bicyclists would crowd the new route and make too much noise. An elderly white man argued that floods of bicyclists would pose a threat to mothers with strollers and "people who like to run in the street." Others claimed the bike boulevard would cause a parking problem due to people driving cars loaded with bicycles to the street. One man more blatantly opined that an increase in bicyclists would attract thieves who would decide to "vacation" on the street. This project threatened the residents' sense of sovereignty, reminding them that they were geographically proximate to less desirable parts of the city.

It was up to them to hold back the flood of outsiders so that their quiet street would remain private property.

The bike enthusiasts at that Long Beach meeting were clearly frustrated with what they saw as NIMBY (not in my backyard) opposition to making commuting by bike safer and more respectable, the end goal of the infrastructure strategy. The sense of injustice here had to do with bicyclists being left out of street design and outrage that such a small use of public resources would be blocked. Nobody said anything about the racist and classist messages encoded in the homeowners' concerns. Was I the only one who noticed them? Riding a bike could make you feel very vulnerable, I knew, but that state of being ended when your ride did. There were other kinds of marginality that did not have those situational limits, and the homeowners wanted to bar people experiencing them from First Street. The bike advocates demonstrated a confident expectation that government power should back up their preferences, including the right to travel in roadways. They probably had more in common with the homeowners who expected the city to protect their enclave than they did with bike users who relied on two wheels due to poverty.

From what I was seeing, most of the people already choosing to bike in Southern California were the kind of undesirable people that the Long Beach homeowners wanted to keep out of their neighborhood. Did these people participate in the bike movement? Was the bike infrastructure strategy designed to address their concerns?

Before I started asking these questions of bike advocates, I found a different movement that was making an explicit connection between racism and sustainable transportation, so I knew I wasn't way off base. Around the same time that I attended the hearing about the bike boulevard, I found a flyer at the Long

Beach Public Library. The flyer was made by a group called the Bus Riders Union/Síndicato de Pasajeros (BRU) and it warned bus riders about the impending cancellations of certain Metro bus routes. I was excited to learn more about who was advocating for the users of stigmatized public transportation.

I attended a regular monthly meeting of the BRU in Koreatown, where I learned the campaign's origins and mission. I also met an older African-American gentleman who turned out to be the person who left the flyer in the Long Beach Public Library. He was very pleased that it had brought someone to the meeting, because he had been placing them in the library for some time without getting a response. This was the first time I encountered simultaneous interpretation, where headsets are available to keep communication inclusive between people speaking multiple languages.

The Labor/Community Strategy Center launched the BRU campaign in response to an L.A. Metro funding crisis in 1994. Faced with a mounting deficit, Metro announced that it was canceling the monthly bus pass service that many low-income riders relied on to meet their transportation needs. Metro was also raising fares overall. At the same time, the transit authority began construction on the Gold Line light rail corridor connecting downtown L.A. to wealthy Pasadena. This revealed a glaring injustice in the allocation of funding: while 94% of users rode the bus, 70% of Metro's funding was being funneled into light rail. According to the BRU, this amounted to transit racism and violated the Civil Rights Act of 1964 Title VI that prohibited discrimination in federally funded projects. To block the fare increase, the BRU successfully sued Metro over the funneling of transportation monies to rail projects rather than bus service. The monthly bus pass program continued, and Metro did not raise fares until 2010.

In the orientation at my first meeting, the organizers explained that the BRU opposed any investment in rail transit because subways and light rail systems were too expensive to distribute equitably across a vast, decentralized county. For the price of every mile of light rail built, six hundred buses could be added, they said. For the price of every mile of subway built, that number jumped to nine hundred. Perhaps most significantly, train systems in L.A. have led to gentrification and rising rents in surrounding neighborhoods, driving the poor out of the city as professionals decide they are tired of commuting in from the San Fernando Valley, as a young black woman at my first meeting put it. The message was that drawing in new users should not come at the cost of those already using sustainable transportation systems.

I would later learn that the BRU has been an influential organizing model for transportation justice groups all over the country. Transportation justice is closely tied to the environmental justice movement, which works to address the fact that more neighborhoods where people of color live have been seen as appropriate sites for waste plants, highways, and other sources of pollution. Beyond the organizing task of enrolling affected individuals in a shared understanding of a local problem they face, a key element of environmental justice is self-determination and meaningful participation in decision-making.[5] There is a recognized need to actively create room for people of color and low-income communities to have different ideas for improving their environments than what might be preferred by an environmentalist mainstream dominated by white participants.

I started thinking about how to connect environmental justice with bicycling. I wanted my investigation of bicycling in L.A. to produce ideas that would improve street culture for its existing

---

5 See "Principles of Environmental Justice" drafted at the First National People of Color
   Environmental Leadership Summit held in 1991 in Washington, D.C.

walkers and bikers, the ones who had to adapt over and over to innovations imposed on them. Plenty of people were already using bikes out of economic necessity; how did they relate to bicycle advocacy, which seemed oriented more toward enrolling future riders? There didn't seem to be an analogue in bicycling for "transit-dependent" or "captive" riders, the public transit terms describing people who do not have the option to drive. The bike movement was more about being "carfree," the descriptor used by people who can afford to drive but choose not to, getting around on bikes, transit, and feet instead.

I started thinking of myself as carfree in 2008, but I have never been transit-dependent. As a teen in a single-parent household I'd relied on buses to get to appointments on my own, but my mother had always had access to the resources to keep a car in running condition. When I gave up my car in college, it was not because I couldn't afford to keep it. I gave it up because life seemed more interesting without it, more of an adventure.

Was it ever like that for the man whose death catalyzed my activism? Did José Umberto Barranco ever ride in a group with friends, gleefully hooting and ringing bells as they filled the street and asserted their right to use the road? Or was he like the other Latino fathers who lived in the neighborhood where I grew up, where riding a bike was a stopgap until a man could buy a truck? There is an ambiguity in street practices like riding a bicycle: one guy does it but wishes he were doing something else, while a few feet away somebody else is doing the exact same thing and loving it. With "captive" and "carfree" indicating such different economic and cultural positions, where do these groups intersect? Do they have a common cause?

The Bus Riders Union was not the intersection point, at least for me. Instead I found an idea for creating a mixed meeting space for captive and carfree cyclists a few months after we'd moved to Long Beach, when Bobby showed me a video posted on the website Streetfilms. That's where we first learned about Bogotá, Colombia's *ciclovía* (bikeway).[6] The nine-minute video said that the event closed over 70 miles of streets to car traffic every Sunday, and it seemed to stretch all over the city. Up to two million people biked or walked leisurely along the route. Aerobics classes and street performances were visible, too, driving home the idea that streets are a social space. The video also explained the logistics for the event, which unlike a marathon or street festival had crossing points for motorized traffic (a "permeable" route). Volunteers and police officers made sure that pedestrians and bicyclists using the ciclovía waited at red lights at these crossing points.

The idea that a street could be transformed without permanent infrastructure besides signage really aligned with what I'd been reading in grad school about the multiple ways people inhabit the same places, and what I'd experienced on group rides. Could this ciclovía thing create a temporary space that transformed car culture? Could we use it to bring together the captive and the carfree?

In June 2008, Bobby and I toured the L.A. Ecovillage, a place I'd heard about at a BRU meeting. Afterwards we stayed to chat with Lois Arkin, the project's founder, and when the ciclovía came up, it turned out she had spent time in Bogotá. She gave me a lead who I could talk to there if I planned to visit. With Bogotá in the back of my mind, I headed to Portland later that month to attend the Toward Carfree Cities Conference, an annual event put on by a group called the World Carfree Network to connect sustainable

---

6 "Ciclovía: Bogotá, Colombia." *Streetfilms*, 2007. I was not the only person impressed with the film. When I contacted the filmmaker, Clarence Eckerson, Jr., he said that a number of graduate students had interviewed him about its impact. The ciclovía film was for years the most viewed video on the site.

transportation movements. The keynote address was given by Gil Peñalosa, the brother of former Bogotá mayor Enrique Peñalosa and the commissioner of parks and recreation during his brother's mayoral term. I had seen him praising Bogotá in the documentary about the ciclovía. A fit, middle-aged man wearing a dapper suit, Peñalosa spoke enthusiastically about a "healthy competition" between New York and Portland, whose city governments were working to start ciclovía-style events.

He was a dynamite speaker, illustrating his commentary with pictures of freeway removal in South Korea and of a woman biking in heels. "Sometimes it is easier to go from bad to great than from good to great," he said, kindly encouraging a group of advocates who often felt overwhelmed by the prospect of changing U.S. street culture. Peñalosa described ciclovía events as "linear parks" that connected wealthy and impoverished districts. He talked about a human right to mobility, and suggested that partnering with public health agencies would create a broader coalition for carfree transportation.

Even though the crowd in the lecture hall was pretty much all white people, they responded warmly to Peñalosa's cheerleading about bicycles being for everyone. The lack of ethnic diversity in the room reminded me of claims that Portland may be bike-friendly, but it's still unwelcoming to people of color. I hadn't thought about it much when I lived there, but I knew that a historically African-American part of the city was the site of tension over gentrification as more young, white people moved into affordable apartments and shared old houses. These bike advocates might want to get everyone on bikes, but where was everybody else? The carfree vision seemed a little one-sided.

It turned out that research on bicycling was also one-sided, as I found when I started the literature review for my dissertation proposal. In one review of bicycle planning research, getting "everyone" on a bike meant expanding bicycle promotion efforts to include not just white male enthusiasts, but also white women and children.[7] That study, by two prominent U.S. bike researchers, mentioned only gender, age, and income as categories that include "everyone." I likewise saw little mention of the economic survival cycling that caught my eye on the streets of Southern California.

It wasn't hard to guess why. Though the editors of the great 2007 collection *Cycling & Society* noted the diversity of reasons why people bike, social scientists studying bicycling have tended to focus on self-identified cyclists. Interested in broadcasting their views, bike enthusiasts are easy to access as research subjects and are willing to speak for a larger group. I wondered if I was the only person noticing this gap, and I was excited to think that I had a scholarly contribution to make. This contrast between who was riding and who was a spokesperson for riding seemed like a great anthropological phenomenon to study. My blood pumped faster with the urgent feeling that I had something to share. I was afraid that other scholars might object to my findings, but fear was a familiar feeling I'd had to push through for as long as I could remember anyway.

To supplement my literature review, I spent the summer of 2008 on fieldwork trips. I traveled to Newark, New York, Washington, D.C. and Atlanta to get a feel for transportation cultures in other cities. In downtown Newark, I saw markets that reminded me of downtown L.A., and was shocked by the proximity of wealthy villages to zones of poverty. In New York City, I noticed how much I'd been trained to respect traffic signals when I felt liberated by jaywalking in crowds. It was the people, not the

---

7 Pucher, J., Buehler, R. 2008. "Cycling for Everyone: Lessons From Europe." Transportation Research Record 2074, 58–65.

traffic infrastructure, who decided the order of the street. In Washington, D.C., I saw Latino riders like in L.A., and for the first time attended a community meeting where residents strategized about how to fight back against gentrification and displacement. That same sense of injustice came out in a play I saw in Atlanta. In that city, I also heard a bus rider yelling at a bus driver about how she should find another job since she was so bad at this one, and her reply made it clear that she felt like a captive too. I processed all these observations on Greyhound buses and Amtrak trains between the cities. In particular I pondered the black/white racial divide that seems taken for granted back east but was unfamiliar to me, coming from my Mexican/white experience.

For my final fieldwork trip of the summer, Bobby and I flew to Bogotá in mid-August 2008. The city was damp and green, with an overcast sky. Nine thousand feet in the Andes, Bogotá has a temperate climate and sees drizzly rain year round. We wandered around the city for three weeks and I never totally adjusted to the narcotic effect the high altitude had on my body. The tiny *tintos* of coffee available everywhere didn't pack the punch of the large cups of strong brew I'd been hooked on since living in the Pacific Northwest.

We stayed with various hosts and learned about local architecture, public cultural resources, and national history. We attended three ciclovías, but beyond those Sundays, we saw few bicyclists using the extensive network of *ciclorutas*, bike paths crisscrossing the city. We saw few bicyclists braving dense, swift traffic in narrow, winding streets. We saw few bicyclists in the hip neighborhoods. Nobody we met had two bikes to lend us for the ciclovía, and no shop offered bicycle rental we could afford. Many of the bikes we did see in use were cargo bikes used to haul scrap for recycling, to vend food, or for other trade purposes. These were too wide to fit between the ciclorutas' occasional bollards. Street vendors offered bike parts on blankets, alongside replacement blender parts, but it seemed like the blenders everyone used to make fresh fruit smoothies were more common than bicycles.

Arts and culture were highly accessible, with free museums and concerts offered by both public and private institutions. We got used to walking past guards with machine guns and having our bags searched each time we entered one of these buildings. At the Museo Quinta de Bolívar, at one time a residence of the great liberator of South America, we watched Michelangelo Antonioni's 1962 film *L'Eclisse*. Clips from Werner Herzog's 1972 *Aguirre, the Wrath of God*, a film about a conquistador's hubris, were used in a historical exhibit on colonial conquest at the Museo Nacional.

Away from the cultural center, the outskirts of the city had ballooned with shantytowns housing *desplazados*, displaced families who had fled their farms due to U.S.-sponsored poison raining down from overhead as a deterrent to coca cultivation. Hundreds of thousands of desplazados were paying the price for the North American appetite for cocaine.

Smelly air pollution made it clear why the ciclovía was popular in a diesel city, and so did the street contempt. I saw it expressed in Bogotá with more intensity than I'd ever witnessed. The cars were smaller than in California, which meant congestion was very thick and composed of tiny vehicles zooming forward in short bursts. Drivers did not yield to pedestrians. Crossing the street meant running unless you were part of a throng. There were no pauses and waves, friendly gestures of road sharing. Motorbikes were more common than bicycles. Taxi drivers regularly ran red lights. All in all, removing motorized traffic during the ciclovía really changed the character of the street because it also removed the time pressure so many drivers working or on their way to work brought into the roadway.

Besides the weekly ciclovía, another method for improving air quality was *pico y placa*, a system that used vehicle license numbers to determine who could drive on what days. One of our hosts told us that people would love to drive more and resented these limits. I found this interesting, since the stance I was starting to understand among sustainable transportation advocates in the United States was that they thought they could convince everyone to *choose* to use cars less. In this city that was getting global attention, they were engineering transportation behavior through autocratic measures we weren't likely to be able to implement in Los Angeles. It wasn't a city full of people joyfully choosing to walk, bike, and ride the bus. It was full of people packed like sardines onto buses who might like to drive more but couldn't because of congestion, regulations, and expense.

In Bogotá, I could see for myself that its complexity as a city, and what made certain interventions work there, were not things we could easily map onto another city in another country. For example, there were city employees and volunteers everywhere we looked. We bought tickets for the Transmilenio bus rapid transit system from people, not machines. The ciclovía was a product of this urban fabric and I wondered what it would look like woven into another one.

We met with Lois Arkin's friend, Anamaria Aristizabal. When she learned of our interest in the ciclovía, she set up a meeting for us with Jaime Ortiz Mariño, who had helped create the event. Jaime invited us to the Bogotá *alcaldía* (mayor's office), where he was minister of domestic transportation. As part of the PRO-CICLA group that also included Fernando Caro Restrepo and Rodrigo Castaño Valencia, Jaime founded the ciclovía in 1974, having returned to Bogotá from undergraduate studies at Case Western Reserve University in Cleveland. The ciclovía waxed and waned over the years. In 1994, Antanus Mockus, a university professor and administrator, ran a successful and unconventional campaign for mayor. Once in charge, he used unusual tactics to improve civic culture in the city, such as hiring mimes to mock aggressive motorists and sponsoring a women's night. The ciclovía grew under Mockus, who used humor to build community. Playful interventions can draw our attention to oppressive but routine behavior; this seemed to be the bogotano theory of change expressed through the ciclovía.

When I asked him via email in May 2013 if the street closures were intended to improve public space and street safety in Bogotá, Jaime clarified that, "in the center [of PRO-CICLA], the bicycle was the symbol and the ciclovía was the instrument we came up with, to open the debate on urban processes and urban form in Colombia in the seventies. Urban safety, betterment of public space, community health and recreation, generation of urban consciousness, development of social integration, etc., were also aims of the event, today proven as end results of the process." Closing the streets to cars and opening them to people was an action whose impacts reached far beyond transportation.

The broader cultural context was key to Jaime's philosophy. In his office, we met a young woman who was a journalist. She explained that people did not bike in Bogotá because they thought looking sweaty was unprofessional. Jaime agreed that the ciclorutas were an inadequate response to the difficulty of getting people on bikes, and that their installation had not attracted significant new users. Street design on its own was not enough if it wasn't tied to programming and cultural events.

Jaime also made sure I understood the postcolonial significance of a transportation idea from South America taking hold in the United States. Colombia followed American highway designs, approximating modernity through automobile infrastructure.

But now, Americans were looking to Colombia for alternatives. Jaime sketched me a map of the world that showed what he called the "global center" (as opposed to "global south") as the "unión de naciones asoleadas" (Union of Sunny Nations). Instead of us sending car culture to Colombia via highway engineering, as had been the trend, they were sending a carfree event north; as Jaime put it, *we* were the "provincianos," and they were "universalizing" us. Jaime's emphasis on postcolonial disruption appealed to me as an alternative to the eurocentric vision I was finding in bike media that promoted Northern European street design. It made a lot more sense to me to try out a bogotano model in Los Angeles than to fantasize about overlaying a Danish or Dutch street network there.

Jaime made photocopies of some newspaper articles from the 1970s covering the early ciclovía events, and I took them home with me as ethnographic artifacts. I left Bogotá convinced that we should give a ciclovía a shot in L.A. and take our place in the Union of Sunny Nations.

Post-Colonial Los Angeles

3

Market day in the Russian colony.

Los Angeles, the northernmost metropolis of América Latina, was full of opportunities for me to wrestle with street culture at the end of the first decade of the twenty-first century, but in retrospect, I've wondered why I felt so gung-ho about meddling with the street culture of a city where I'd never lived before. Why did I think Los Angeles was mine? It was in part because I had been raised to see L.A. as a cultural center where Mexican-American identity was so strong that there was room in it for a half-white person like me. I thought of it this way because my older sister Gia went to UC Berkeley and minored in Chicano Studies.

Chicano, Chicana or, being gender-inclusive, Chicanx, describes a lot of different cultural styles, with the link in-between being some blending of Mexican and U.S. traditions. Some Chicanxs speak only English and have no ties to the Mexico their great-great-grandparents left. Others go home to a *ranchito* every summer. The place Gia taught me to associate with this Chicana identity was Los Angeles.

Beyond Chicanxs, there are many more groups who have shaped L.A. and made it their home, including many immigrants from other Latin American countries with whom we share the identifier Latina/Latino/Latinx. Many Latinxs are racially mixed, *mestizos* whose ancestry includes Indigenous Americans, European settlers, and African slaves. This means we don't fit neatly on one side or the other of the black/white dichotomy that has tended to shape analysis of race relations in this country, although mixed people have been part and parcel of the colonial project to maintain division between races and classes.

That project of division has had major effects on the development, growth, and mythologizing of my homeland, and we understand it differently based on what group's history we center in our narratives. I built on my sister's lessons in college when I studied the colonial history of race and place in Orange County, continuing my focus on the Mexican legacy in California. This focus is present in the story I share here, which I mostly got from books.

The Spanish settlers who arrived in the late 1700s were the first to impose a eurocentric racial hierarchy on this land and its people. To get a feel for what this imposition entailed, consider the following account of a forcible conversion that historian A.H. Fitch included in his 1914 book on the Franciscan leader Junípero Serra.[8] After traveling for several days without blessing any "wild" Indians, the mission party spotted some potential *conversos* (converts). Fitch drew this from Serra's own journal:

> Two Gentiles were again visible on the same height, and our Indians—shrewder than yesterday, went to catch them with caution that they should not escape them. And although one fled from between their hands they caught the other. They tied him, and it was all necessary, for even bound he defended himself that they should not bring him and flung himself upon the ground with such violence that he scraped and bruised his thighs and knees. But at last they brought him. They set him before me' ...After making the sign of the cross over him, Junípero untied him, still 'most frightened and disturbed.'

8 Fitch, A.H. 1914. *Junipero Serra: The Man and His Work*.

Tying people up to save their souls. Seizing their land and enslaving them to work it. This is the violence that gets glossed as "contact." It was a contact so brutal that we've been shrinking from it ever since.

Once forcible baptisms had been performed, the missionaries identified people by the missions that had claimed them: Tongva became Gabrieliños, associated with Mission San Gabriel, and the Acjachemen at Mission San Juan Capistrano became Juaneños. If *conversos* fled, soldiers would hunt them down and bring them back. Spiritual conversion was the central rationale for their subjugation, but it had to be realized through physical means.

Prior to missionization, the Native peoples in this temperate zone had inhabited stick dwellings called *wikiups*, burning them down and building fresh ones every so often. The Spanish forced them to construct and live in adobe barracks and houses. According to historian Sherburne F. Cook, housing conversos in unfamiliar and reportedly filthy dormitories was part of the project to isolate the Natives from their way of life, a rupture the padres considered necessary to the conversion process.[9] At missions, men and women conversos were forced to sleep in different dormitories to control their supposed promiscuity. This arrangement did not protect Native women from what the writer Carey McWilliams called the "scrofulous Spanish soldiery."[10] Venereal disease was widespread. During the years of mission rule from 1769 to 1834, Franciscan friars punished Native women who miscarried, suspecting them of aborting their children. Maybe these women thought it was more humane to end their race rather than see their children subjected to mission life.

While mission settlements carried out the religious project of controlling Native life and labor, soldiers and other colonizers

9 Cook, Sherburne F. 1976. *The Conflict Between the California Indian and White Civilization.*
10 McWilliams, Carey. 1973. *Southern California: An Island on the Land.*

spread out across the region and built trading posts under military rather than religious control. Over several years, they established sites within a day's ride of each other up the coast as far as what became San Francisco, baptizing the land with Catholic names. Stopping at the Tongva village of Yangna along a river, Spanish soldiers gave the water the name *Nuestra señora la reina de los angeles de porciúncula* (Our lady queen of the angels of the small portion), commemorating the Catholic feast day of August 2. On September 4, 1781, a group of eleven families left the San Gabriel Mission and traveled ten miles to found a pueblo at Yangna, what they called *El pueblo de nuestra señora la reina de los angeles* after the river they'd already christened. Historian Richard Griswold de Castillo reported that the record lists the founding party as mostly mestizos, though later families preferred to call themselves pure blood descendants of Spanish conquistadors.[11] The 1781 pueblo was founded as a secular village rather than a religious mission but also used Native slave labor. In order to maintain their vision of a higher life at missions, the padres made the sacred space of the mission off limits to the profane pueblo Natives, McWilliams reported.

The Río de Porciúncula, as the Spanish and then Mexican settlers called what is today named the Los Angeles River, flooded every ten years or so and tended to shift its course dramatically. This made the land immediately adjacent to the river unsuitable for development, so the pueblo resettled a short distance away from the river on higher ground, near the area today called Placita Olvera. Felipe de Neve, governor of the Spanish territory of Las Californias and a founder of Los Angeles pueblo, created a gridded town plan to govern the growth of the settlement based on the Law of the Indies, which was itself based on an urban model that

11 Griswold del Castillo, Richard. 1979. *The Los Angeles Barrio, 1850-1890: A Social History*.

dates back to Vitruvius of the Roman Empire. This urban grid sits under central Los Angeles today.

Royal land grants to soldiers carved the region into enormous ranchos soon after Spanish settlement began. In 1784, the land east of the L.A. River became José Maria Verdugo's Rancho San Rafael, and the land west of the river became Manuel Nieto's Rancho Los Nietos. When Mexico declared independence from Spain in 1810, the ruling class in Alta California remained in power. These *hispano* (claiming direct Spanish rather than mestizo descent) families who raised cattle for the hide and tallow trade called themselves *gente de razón* (civilized people) and Californios. They sat atop the social hierarchy, with mestizos below them and indios at the bottom.

What this hierarchy meant for the distribution of resources can be seen in the transition of mission land from church to secular hands. In its constitution of 1824, the Mexican government claimed all Catholic Church property for itself. According to historian Leonard Pitt, the new government at Monterey on the Alta California central coast claimed they were restructuring the missions as secular settlements of indios, but in effect they liquidated mission resources and sold them off to Californios.[12] This process continued until the last sale of mission property in May 1845 and opened much more land for Mexican settlement. Roughly forced into mission life, the Natives now had to accept secular subjugation under a social order that despised them. It was a thorough dispossession, and one that apparently seemed completely civilized to those it benefited.

In the first half of the nineteenth century, the population grew very slowly, with Native peoples dying out through missionization

12 Pitt, Leonard. 1970. *The Decline of the Californios: A Social History of the Spanish-Speaking Californians, 1846-1890.*

and mestizo laborers and soldiers emigrating from others parts of Mexico. Prisoners were sent to this remote territory as well, which felt a world away from the country's mainland and so developed its own culture in isolation. Some of those who migrated to the region were fortune seekers from Europe or the new United States far to the east. A few of these men married into wealthy families and assimilated, assuming the gente de razón title "Don" and adopting Spanish pronunciation of their names. John Forster became Don Juan Forster when he married into the Pico family, Abel Stearns became Don Abél Stearns when he married into the Bandini family. Forster eventually purchased the San Juan Mission and his family lived there for a time in the late nineteenth century. I went to a middle school named after his son, and Forsters wearing cowboy hats presided over heritage festivals in San Juan when I was a kid.

The historian Pitt used American sailor Richard Henry Dana's 1840 observations of the region to argue that to these immigrants, "California was not a place of real men sustained by traditions, institutions, and aspirations. Instead, it became an imaginary construct of two-dimensional characters moving about a pleasant landscape, 'without any apparent object' in life." Lacking respect for the culture they had married into, some of these immigrants eased the transition of power from Mexico to the United States. Don Juan Forster aided U.S. troops when they invaded Alta California in 1846. His brother-in-law, Pío de Jesús Pico, would be the last Mexican governor.

California became U.S. territory upon the signing of the Treaty of Guadalupe Hidalgo in 1848. It seems that the Californios did not expect much to change with this territorial conquest. They were far from the seat of power in Mexico City and were accustomed to self-rule. Most importantly, according to the terms of the treaty, the new government would recognize private landholdings. (The

Natives, having already been neutralized as a collective force through decades of genocidal violence, didn't rate the diplomacy of treaties and many coastal tribes continue to await federal recognition today.) However, in order to keep a property title, the United States required submission of proof of a claim to land. Many families who failed to produce these documents lost their property by going into debt during litigation while trying to fight the claims of American squatters. As historian Lisbeth Haas has pointed out, this did not turn them into populists who renounced their sense of superiority.[13] The Californios apparently did not see history repeating itself when they were conquered by a social structure that placed them in the same category of insignificance where they placed their own laborers. Rancho by rancho, plot by plot, Anglos took control of the land and began parceling it first into farms and then into today's sprawling residential suburbs. Deep in the seas of subdivisions, there are parks where old adobes rot.

Slowly the Mexican region became an Anglo one. The Anglo population became the majority after 1860, and it was not until 2015 that California again saw a Latino majority in the state. (We have proven to be remarkably skilled at repopulating, both through native birth and in-migration.) The incoming conquerors didn't believe in the Californios' distinction from the darker masses who had toiled under them during feudal rule and the Californio elite collapsed into a barrio underclass over time. In 1870, the former Governor Pico built a luxurious hotel on the west side of Placita Olvera and spent ten years serving wealthy guests in opulent settings before losing the hotel to foreclosure. Pico died penniless while his brother-in-law Don Juan Forster prospered

---

13 Haas, Lisbeth. 2000. "Modesta Avila vs. the Railroad and Other Stories about Conquest, Resistance, and Village Life." In *Chicana Literary and Artistic Expressions: Culture and Society in Dialogue.*

in San Juan. Other formerly wealthy families became street food vendors and scraped by in American Los Angeles.

Army Lieutenant Edward O.C. Ord expanded Felipe de Neve's original plan for Los Angeles in 1849 after California became a U.S. territory, and the city grew block by block in the second half of the nineteenth century. Wooden frame and then brick buildings replaced the adobes that had replaced the stick huts, and an urban center emerged. White inhabitants called the original pueblo area Sonora Town, Little Mexico, Chinatown, and Nigger Alley. Many people from the northern Mexican state of Sonora came to California during the Gold Rush, and they got lumped in with the mestizos, Natives, and Californios. Calling the original pueblo Sonora Town labeled its inhabitants foreigners, Mexicans, interlopers rather than members of a longstanding community in that place. Subsequent populations, such as the Chinese community that grew in L.A. after 1850, and the Japanese immigrants who came around 1900, also settled in this area.

As the gente de razón lost power and their adobe estates crumbled, newer settlers romanticized their way of life through a pastoral vision of distant, gently-tolling mission bells, and pious indios bent in prayer or in farmwork. Padres, dons, and conversos lived in harmony, while on mission-adjacent ranchos beautiful señoritas danced with handsome men whose spurs flashed as they kicked. This nostalgic mythology reinforced the invisibility of the living people on which these images were based. McWilliams characterized this as a division between the "sacred" dead past and the "profane" living remnants who sullied the city, commenting that "the sacred side of this tradition, as represented in the beautifully restored Mission, is worshiped by all alike without regard to caste, class, or religious affiliation. The restored Mission is a much better, less embarrassing symbol of the past than the Mexican field worker or the ragamuffin *pachucos* of Los

Angeles." The living bodies of the undesirables had been divorced from the fantasized past that would be sold to incoming millions, but they didn't go away.

The Southern Pacific Railroad reached Los Angeles in 1881, opening the region to tourism and immigration at a scale impossible beforehand. The region led the country in growth between 1890 and 1930, with its population increasing from eleven thousand residents in 1890 to 1.2 million by the beginning of the Great Depression. Downtown grew southward and westward along the river and the Santa Monica Mountains, but beyond the dense buildings of downtown, streetcars allowed people to live away from the bustling center. Los Angeles' power elite wanted to achieve a Garden City, which spread outwards rather than upwards. Developers built railway lines to neighborhoods being parceled, constructed, and sold by the same companies. The Pacific Electric Railway, incorporated by Henry Huntington, and the Los Angeles Railway, purchased by Huntington, served the region from 1901 until they stopped service in 1961. At one point it was the largest interurban system in the world.

The subdivisions' attraction was in part their distance from industrial pollution, but L.A.'s diversity was definitely seen as something negative too. Access to racial isolation was one of suburban development's major selling points.[14] This style of development was backed up by early urban sociology, which framed social mixing as unhealthy. Strangers, Georg Simmel argued in 1903, experience "a slight aversion, a mutual strangeness and repulsion, which will break into hatred and fight at the moment of a closer contact, however caused."[15] They developed what he called a "blasé attitude" as a way to cope with exposure to

14 Historian Kenneth T. Jackson's book *Crabgrass Frontier* provides a comprehensive overview of the social distance touted as a selling point of suburbanization, and M.P. Baumgartner's *The Moral Order of a Suburb* outlines the social distance that suburban living structured into daily life.

15 Simmel, Georg. 1964. "The Stranger." In *The Sociology of Georg Simmel*.

so many others. The blasé attitude was seen as a product of urban life as opposed to rural life, and a sign of the moral decay that people went through by living in cities. Racially mixed zones were corrupting and unhealthy. While this aversion could have been problematized, the planning and development experts of the time naturalized it. As a prominent urban planner explained in 1926, decentralization made sense because "the natural reaction of a population anywhere is to spread out in sub-centers, to build up small communities and business districts, to get the advantages of the city without its very apparent disadvantages."[16]

Because streetcars had already created distance between homes and work, and because cars offered an alternative to perceived corruption in the streetcar companies, L.A. residents adopted driving first in the country.[17] Those who could afford to purchase cars could travel where and when they pleased, without being beholden to a timetable or crammed into a hot space with many other bodies. On streetcars you had to mingle with classes and races you might prefer to avoid; the car granted the freedom to separate. In 1926, the *Examiner* newspaper asked that, "if there is ever to be a union station . . . let it at least not be located between Chinatown and Little Mexico.' Which would the public prefer, the paper asked, a 'depot in [the] Chinese district, or no more grade crossings?"[18] Traffic congestion was a pain, but so was having to spend time with ethnics. In a racist and classist society, being able to distance your family from people of color and the poor is just common sense to those who can afford to do it. Building social exclusion into the housing landscape meant geographically isolating precious kids from bad people. Cars weren't just vehicles for upward mobility; they were getaway cars.

16 Quoted in Bottles 1987.
17 I've found Scott Bottles' 1987 book *Los Angeles and the Automobile* to be very helpful for understanding the transition from streetcars to private cars, and I'm following his argument here.
18 Quoted in Bottles 1987.

The drop in ridership ruined the streetcar companies, which were not necessarily profitable enterprises on their own so much as they were conduits to housing tracts. The demise of the streetcars created a sharp divide between those who could afford to drive and those who could not. Traveling inside of private cars became a mark of distinction and traveling outside of private cars became a mark of shame.[19] The people glossed as "very apparent disadvantages" by that 1920s planner were residentially confined as much as possible through redlining and other well-documented practices of keeping people of color out of even government-subsidized new housing. By the 1950s, decentralized mobility had drained power from downtown Los Angeles, so landed interests there pushed for more and more freeway access and large-scale redevelopment of blighted neighborhoods. At that time, a city could call a neighborhood blighted and get federal funding to tear it down. Blocks full of people were informed that they were slumdwellers who needed to be rehomed like inconvenient pets. The myth of miasma continued in the notion that by tearing down the buildings these people inhabited, and building new ones, the slum would be gone.

Most of that planned housing never got built. Urban renewal became another mechanism for removing people of color, like deportation (Mexican-Americans during the Great Depression) or internment (Japanese-Americans during World War II). As geographer Laura Pulido put it in her 2006 book *Black, Brown, Yellow, and Left*, "people of color were simply not part of the Southern California dream that millions of whites wished to buy into." But unlike these more explicitly racialized policies, urban renewal worked through manipulating the streets and buildings people of color inhabited, making their removal a precondition

---

19 L.A. writer and educator Sikivu Hutchinson published a great essay called "Waiting for the Bus" detailing this divide in the journal *Social Text* in 2000.

for improved cities. This deeply embedded and often obscured racism sits at the heart of the gentrification occurring today.

Today, nostalgia for the streetcars is much more widespread than dialogue about the racial divides that car travel reinforced, and while it has become common to decry modernist urban planning as a short-sighted project that locked us into exurban sprawl, I find that critics seem uninterested in what trauma this one-sided planning caused to the people who could not afford to comply with car culture. How did they react to the shame of traveling wrong, traveling insecurely? How does that trauma shape attitudes toward public transit, biking, and walking in Southern California today? What is it like to be blight? To be the thing that blocks Progress, to be the thing that needs to be removed so that others can be healthy. Surely that takes an emotional toll. And what would make a person feel better faster: taking down car culture, or just getting inside a car?

One aspect of car-dependent development seems to be that those who grow up benefiting from its inequitable distribution of education and wealth can find fault with it more easily than the people who have to bear its burdens. For example, historian Eric Avila's 2014 book *The Folklore of the Freeway* covers how freeway removal, a cause célèbre for white urbanists, oversimplifies how the gashes highways cut through urban neighborhoods healed over in places like New Orleans, Barrio Logan in San Diego, and Boyle Heights in L.A., where communities turned retaining walls and overpasses into spaces for cultural expression.

Much of that public art grew out of the political and cultural efforts of the Chicano Movement, which blossomed around the southwest starting in the 1960s. Chicanx muralists drew on a public art tradition that had developed in Mexico several decades earlier, when exalting the concept of *mestizaje* (racial hybridity) had become a government-sponsored cultural project. Cultural elites like the artist Diego Rivera produced politicized representations of Indigenous life and history as nationalist symbols of strength. In an essay on mestizaje, anthropologist Ana María Alonso reported that the celebration of Indigenous cultures had been growing since late nineteenth-century Mexico, when "postcolonial revisionist history exalted the dead Indians of the past [while] their descendants, Indians and *indomestizos*, continued to be stigmatized."[20] The Mexican artists of Rivera's milieu in part challenged a sacred landscapes/profane bodies split similar to the one in California, and in part continued it. From what I can tell, it was the working-class Chicano Movement that went further in breaking down the barrier between who carried the folk culture and who created artistic representations of it. Being hybrid, being mestizo, Chicanx artists expressed how mixed roots made us rich, not inferior. And L.A. was at the center of it, deep in Aztlán, the mythical homeland of the Mexica.

Despite decades of communities of color organizing to celebrate their cultures in the face of white supremacy, all the segregation embedded in the development pattern means it's still possible for us to live in very different versions of L.A., which is why I'm careful to clarify how my family's perspective on race shaped mine. It's why there can be a "nobody walks in L.A." image even though bustling urban life has existed here since the late nineteenth century. Because I already had an inkling of how race, class, and mobility shaped Los Angeles, I could see that the street contempt I started studying in 2007 had deep roots. Transportation systems get us *to*, and they take us away *from*.

When my sister taught me about California's colonial history, she made sure I understood that the racial discrimination

---

20 From Alonso's 2004 article "Conforming Disconformity: 'Mestizaje,' Hybridity, and the Aesthetics of Mexican Nationalism" published in the journal *American Anthropologist*.

underpinning the successive land grabs had never gone away. It was in the ground we walked on and in the mindset that drove 1990s ballot measures against immigrants like Propositions 187 and 227.[21] To make me feel more connected to Mexican history in California, Gia occasionally took small me to Los Angeles on the train. We would depart from San Juan Capistrano's station on Los Rios, passing by the nineteenth-century shacks and adobes that now house boutiques and cafés. Upon arriving at Union Station in L.A., we would cross Alameda and spend hours on Olvera Street, a cobblestone alley lined with vendors hawking leather goods and other items that smelled like trips to see family in Tijuana, on their side of the border.

I loved visiting Olvera Street's folkloric spectacle. At one end of the alley was the approximate location of the original Spanish town square, now called la Placita Olvera. There, a gazebo housed mariachi bands and Aztec dancers dressed in loincloths and percussive anklets shook feathers at us. Along the alley were various old buildings that housed shops, museums, restaurants; white-walled adobes with heavy wood beams like the ones back home in San Juan. The Pico Hotel was still there, but it was always closed for restoration when my sister and I visited Olvera Street. Once, we peeked into the windows and were startled to see crudely molded plaster horses, with straining, fiery nostrils and wild eyes, rearing up in the center of the room. Maybe the disused hotel was being used as theater storage.

This was Los Angeles, my sister told me, and we should be proud to be Chicanas here. We were only distantly related to the prominent *Californio* Lugo family who prospered here in the rancho period

---

21 This region's romanticized past, combined with the never-ceasing inflow of new immigrants, makes for all kinds of contradictions. Before I was born, my family used to take part in an annual pageant called Los Cristianitos (the little Christians) held in the hills outside of San Juan that depicted Native conversion. My older siblings had roles as children who gratefully received baptism from a wise padre, and my parents played Mexican folk ballads during intermission.

from 1810 to 1850, but neither were we foreigners in Chicano Los Angeles. At home in segregated south Orange County, our mixed family didn't fit in. Los Angeles had room for us, and I counted on finding this old sense of comfort when I moved here in 2008.

Living in the Plains of Id

4

It was a testament to the Chicano Movement's efforts to institutionalize its culture that I could feel like I was moving to a Chicanx city without actually knowing anyone in that movement or community. So, even though my background drew me to analyze the relationship between race and transportation in the Latinx metropolis, it was my sense of urgency around environmental sustainability that determined where I landed in Los Angeles: Koreatown, because that was where the L.A. Ecovillage (LAEV) intentional community was located.

Koreatown is a central Los Angeles neighborhood that spread north and south of Wilshire Boulevard between the adjacent neighborhoods of MacArthur Park and Hancock Park. Its neighbor to the east, MacArthur Park, was a hub for the Central American immigrant community when I showed up in 2008. Its neighbor to the west, Hancock Park, was much whiter and filled with large, well-maintained mansions. Koreatown was the transitional zone in-between, very diverse in terms of housing density and its residents. The Korean business community gave the neighborhood its official name, but it housed immigrant families from all over the world, with Latin American and Asian sending countries predominant.

You could walk down block after block of large apartment buildings, navigating sidewalks occasionally piled with the furniture abandoned by tenants who had to leave in a hurry. The older buildings from the 1920s and 30s often had ornate stucco facade work, beautiful under layers of grime. One by one they were starting to get rehabbed, especially toward the Hancock Park side of the neighborhood where the apartment buildings transitioned into small Craftsman bungalows before giving way to the large lawns and sycamore-lined streets of the wealthy enclave. On the eastern edge, we had to make do with dying palms whose crowns high above us offered little shade. I had visited the neighborhood before because one of my sisters had lived there, but I did not expect there to be an ecological-living project a few blocks down from the $3 clothing warehouse and the Filipino fried chicken franchise.

After years of planning and organizing, the L.A. Ecovillage started its existence as a housing community in 1996, when its organizers bought a 40-unit building just off a commercial corridor up which the anger of the 1992 riots (or the uprising, as locals call it) spread almost as far north as Hollywood. A few years later they bought a smaller building next door, adding family-size units to the project. As I'd heard on my tour at the beginning of the summer, the ecovillage concept aimed to create human-scaled, full-featured demonstration communities that integrated social, economic, and ecological systems and minimized waste. Most U.S. ecovillages were in rural settings and required that residents become property owners. This urban ecovillage was unusual, both in its location and the racial and income diversity of its inhabitants. Not everyone at LAEV was an expert on sustainability systems, but the members who lived in its two 1920s apartment buildings surrounded by gardens and trees shared the belief that spending time together in community could help repair the damage humans have done to our planet.

Rough around the edges, the buildings felt occupied and open at the same time. Standing on the sidewalk in front of the large,

U-shaped main building, passersby could see a riot of plants, both tended and wild, growing in the yard between the fence and the beige stucco building. The sidewalk itself looked different too, the product of a city-sponsored attempt to allow rainwater to reach the underlying soil through permeable concrete. Through the gate was a glimpse of the tiled lobby, with green-trimmed French doors open to a sunny courtyard. The courtyard filled the space between the building's wings with trees, gardens, and a chicken coop. As a frequent meeting space for community groups and projects, the lobby, courtyard, and community meeting room upstairs at LAEV were more public than private.

LAEV also differed from the typical ecovillage in that it was a retrofit rather than a new building project. One way to be sustainable was to start with technologically advanced systems; another was to adapt what you had. At the Ecovillage, DIY (do it yourself) was the ruling ethos. Many apartments had been completely overhauled. Some were filled with garbage and broken appliances when the building was purchased. Existing residents stayed on, while the other units filled slowly over time as they were rehabbed (through ecologically sound methods when possible). As more people moved in, the intentional community formalized a membership process to socialize potential new residents and gauge their interest in ecological sustainability. The place felt like a cross between an SRO and a hippie commune, a green oasis in a big, dirty city that reminded me of the eco culture I'd known in the Pacific Northwest. I liked the overall vibe, but the main reason why I wanted to become an ecovillager was that people there didn't react to me like I was a jerk for being a bike commuter.

Many ecovillagers chose to live carfree, though not all rode bikes. With both express and local buses running 24 hours a day on Vermont Avenue and a short walk to the Vermont/Beverly subway station that opened in 1999, LAEV was strategically sited to enable getting around L.A. on foot and public transportation. There were four grocery stores within walking distance, for example. For some ecovillagers, getting around on transit or bikes didn't have a particular significance; it was just a simple step toward reducing one's ecological impact, like taking tote bags to the grocery store or recycling. For others, bicycling was at the center of their social and professional lives.

One such ecovillager was bike messenger and musician Randy Metz, who had been living at LAEV since the early 2000s. Randy showed to me how to ride to places like the Hollywood Farmer's Market and Heritage Square in Lincoln Heights. He didn't take his cue from city-designated routes such as streets with bike lanes. Instead, over many years of riding he had amassed a detailed knowledge of back alleys and shortcuts that could take him all over the city. Randy's routes avoided major streets, zigzagging through the parallel neighborhood streets of the central L.A. urban grid. Randy expressed a lot of satisfaction with his knowledge of the city, and his eyes gleamed gleefully when he talked about flying through the city on a bike or skateboard.

On the one hand, bicyclists could hack the streets, passing through openings that a person might not notice from a car or a bus. On the other hand, they faced harsh treatment from fellow road users traveling by car; this contrast was part of what pushed bicycle users to organize as activists. And when I say "harsh treatment," I don't mean honking horns and flipping the bird. Everyone I know who advocates for bicyling has been hurt by a car, or knows someone who has been hurt or killed by a car. Zooming out, we all know someone who has been hurt or taken from us by vehicular violence. What made bike advocates different was that something had shaken us out of seeing this violence as routine. Being carfree wasn't just about bikes; it was a response to an overall harmful and destructive system.

I didn't know it when I decided to enter the membership process there, but the Ecovillage had been a central site where the direct action and fun of group rides developed into political advocacy around bikes in Los Angeles. In the late 1990s, it became a community hub for people who had met through L.A.'s Critical Mass. Critical Mass is a group bike ride that started in San Francisco in 1992 and has spread to cities across the world. On the last Friday of each month, Masses converge at appointed times and places and people take a meandering ride through the city, becoming a living, mobile statement about bicycling as transportation.[22] The event's early participants were committed to a nonhierarchical ethos for the ride, so it has no official spokesperson, but the writer Chris Carlsson has been a steward of its history. Early in 2009, I saw Carlsson speak at LAEV and he gave me a placard with the statement "Bicycling: A Quiet Statement Against Oil Wars." In the work of bike writers like Carlsson and cultural studies scholar Zack Furness, I found a message that matched my own hunch: riding a bike could be a rejection of the reckless exploitation of human and natural resources justified by global capitalism. The Ecovillage nurtured this view as well.

L.A.'s Critical Mass had been organized in 1997 by Ron Milam, a young white man who had grown up in L.A. and went to college in Oregon, after which he interned with a prominent bike organization in Portland.[23] As the ride grew to several dozen participants, a core group decided to launch a bicycle advocacy organization that would promote bicycling through transportation planning at the city level, something beyond the scope of the grassroots ride. This led to the formation of the Los Angeles County Bicycle Coalition (LACBC) in 1998 and the start

---

22 For a collection of essays on the ride's significance in cities around the world see *Critical Mass: Bicycling's Defiant Celebration* (2002).

23 I interviewed the founders of L.A. Critical Mass for a chapter in the 2012 book *Shift Happens! Critical Mass at 20.*

of an organized effort to retrofit L.A. streets to accommodate bicycling as a legitimate mode of transportation.

Ron and another LACBC founder, Joe Linton, had both moved into the Ecovillage, where Lois Arkin and others were living carfree. Jimmy Lizama, an artist and early participant in Critical Mass and LACBC, also became an ecovillager, and there he turned a kitchen in one of the uninhabitable apartments into a workshop where he and his friends taught themselves bike repair. This became the Bicycle Kitchen/Bicicocina repair cooperative, which eventually moved to its own storefront in East Hollywood. As journalist Damien Newton reported, the camaraderie felt by folks at the Kitchen led to small group rides, eventually becoming the Midnight Ridazz in 2004.[24] At the first potluck Bobby and I attended at the Ecovillage in September 2008, we talked about our recent trip to Bogotá and asked if the ecovillagers knew anyone working on a ciclovía effort. They invited us to an LACBC board meeting the following Wednesday, and my L.A. fieldwork was off to a good start.

From September 2008 to March 2009, while we went through the Ecovillage membership process, Bobby and I lived five blocks away from LAEV on the northern edge of Koreatown, in a studio apartment with walls like lemon cream pie—yellow topped with white moldings. Laminate flooring and an air conditioning unit to guard us against Southern California's autumn heat partially made up for the cockroach population in our kitchen. Due to the high rents in the central city, most of the other units housed entire families, and the building's front porch was a gathering spot for the many teens living there. I chatted with women neighbors, greeting them with *buenas*, the slang I had learned during fieldwork in Bogotá the past summer. These Central American

---

24 Damien Newton interviewed the founders of Midnight Ridazz in 2009 for the website *LA Streetsblog*.

women were friendly, if guarded. A young woman across the hall seemed to be having trouble with her boyfriend. Her small son sometimes toddled into our apartment.

Bobby was the only white person who lived in the building, but he and I were not the only bicycle users. Mountain bikes were locked up to railings inside and behind the building. Most of the people who lived in our building could be seen walking and using public transit in the neighborhood. Like the people I had observed biking in Long Beach, these cyclists tended to stay on major streets and avoided drivers' aggression by riding on sidewalks. Bobby and I got familiar with our new neighborhood by walking and biking around, visiting the local Latino grocery store, and eating out, choosing from Vietnamese, Korean, Salvadoran, Mexican, Hawaiian, Bangladeshi, and 24-hour donut restaurants.

Koreatown was much rougher than anywhere I'd lived before, but its public spaces felt familiarly Latino. Living in central L.A. drove home how racist it was that my childhood neighborhood, the Villas, had been called a ghetto. We'd had suburban swimming pools and green lawns, but we had the same Latina mothers bundling kids down the sidewalk, *paletero* ice cream carts, and food trucks that gave my new neighborhood its character. Calling the Villas a ghetto was a judgment against its people; we were what made it a bad place to live.

The city had more tangible dangers, I learned soon after we moved in. Amidst the strip malls on bustling Third Street, there was a defunct dentist's office. In front of the closed office, there lived a large man, his scent and scattered belongings marking the block. I remember wrinkling my nose at the smell of unwashed human, thinking I should avoid his block in the future. A few weeks after I had made this observation, a carload of men stopped in front of this man, doused him in gasoline, and lit him on fire. Then they drove away, leaving him to die.

Some local women organized a vigil for the dead man, who they had known for years. Bobby and I walked our bikes over to the vigil with new acquaintances from the Ecovillage. Standing on the edge of a crowd made up mostly of Latina women and children, we attracted the attention of a reporter for a local weekly paper. She quickly transitioned from covering the vigil to asking about our bikes, and whether we ever went on Midnight Ridazz group rides. Her colorful glasses and bright attire marked her as someone interested in urban bike culture. I felt embarrassed by my ability to be so close to but separate from the spectacle of grief and outrage surrounding the awful death of this stranger. Something seemed off.

I think it was that people with our education and economic security weren't supposed to be out on that street; we were supposed to be passing through that neighborhood in cars, on our way to some restaurant or nightclub. There were two transportation worlds in the same place and time. In one, the extensive transit network and the urban street grid made getting around without a car possible, if not always comfortable. In the other, alternatives to driving simply didn't exist, and neither did all the people outside of cars and the public spaces they occupied.

For many, many decades the car paradigm has dominated the image of L.A. transportation. Despite the fact that there has never been a time when everyone could afford to drive, the enclosed environment of the private automobile became an adequate viewpoint from which to characterize all L.A. The view from the driver's seat even became a fetish object, through architectural studies such as Reyner Banham's 1971 *Los Angeles: Architecture of Four Ecologies*. That book celebrated car-centered sprawl and landscapes designed to accommodate driving, especially what Banham, borrowing the name of a Disneyland ride, called Autopia.

Autopia was one of four landscapes that Banham named as characteristic of Los Angeles, the others being Surfurbia, the Foothills, and the Plains of Id. These were defined by geography, with Surfurbia describing the suburban towns along the coast, and the Foothills describing the homes on stilts clinging to the Santa Monica Mountains that stretch from Malibu to downtown L.A. The Plains of Id described what Banham called the vast, "Anywheresville" stretch between Surfurbia and the Foothills. Autopia, finally, referred to the technological triumph of L.A.'s network of freeways.

I was finding that Autopia was not geographically fixed; it described the mobile mentality that every place is best accessed by car. Car culture created the expectation that driving should be convenient even in Los Angeles' dense urban core, and sshh don't talk about it, but Angelenos also drove after drinking. Driving, or being driven, was the way to go, regardless of whether you were trying to get to a foodie hotspot downtown or to a Chinese restaurant in suburban Alhambra. Drivers had a hard time admitting that they could be in the wrong, because in L.A. driving made you right. It's how you were *supposed* to travel. Cultural commentary like Banham's, which was having a revival when I moved to Los Angeles, helped to fetishize car travel as the authentic L.A. experience.

Once it got going, car culture really sold itself, because having the money to get into a car was a way to escape the worthlessness of being outside of one. This worthlessness was documented incidentally in Banham's 1972 BBC film, *Reyner Banham Loves Los Angeles*. In the film, he narrates his journey through L.A. from behind the wheel of a car, accompanied by a proto-GPS system called Baede-Kar that tells him where to go. When Banham visits the Watts Towers, the film's narration confirms to a presumed white viewing audience that it is unusual to go to Watts, but it's worth it to see the outsider art landmark. Banham cuts off black pedestrians with his car while telling the viewer his interpretation of the cultural value of this place whose actual inhabitants he does not meet. For several minutes, the film plays jazz over aerial shots and spinning close ups of the mosaic towers. Then it's back to the freeway.

Referencing Banham's four ecologies, urban theorist Margaret Crawford called this satisfaction with observing from the interior space of a car the "fifth ecology" of fantasy, fundamentally enabled by Autopia.[25] She likens traveling in a car to watching television: "we move through the city without disturbing it or it disturbing us." As "a strictly visual event that does not invite participation," driving acclimates us to gazing through our windshields at static objects, not moving life. Maybe it's a kind of survival response; believing ourselves to be weaving through an obstacle course keeps our nerves in better condition than recognizing that anything traveling with or against us could cross our path at any moment.

I think of Banham's work as freeway flânerie. *Flânerie*, or drifting, is a mode of urban observation that is in some ways similar to the ethnographic approach that anthropologists use. It was my primary method for getting to know Los Angeles, using my bike and my feet and my senses to learn what made it itself. I read a lot about flânerie in my academic studies and found it to be a good way to describe my own research methods, because it reminded me of the kind of wandering I'd been doing since I was a teen,

---

25 The quotes are from Crawford's 1992 essay "The Fifth Ecology: Fantasy, the Automobile, and Los Angeles" from the book *The Car and the City: The Automobile, the Built Environment, and Daily Urban Life* edited by herself and Martin Wachs.

walking around San Juan, riding the bus around Portland, and now riding a bike in Los Angeles. You witness place differently when you focus on being in motion rather than on your destination.

There's also something exhilarating in it, which Virgina Woolf illustrated in *Mrs. Dalloway*, where she sent one character off on a drift:

> And Elizabeth waited in Victoria Street for an omnibus. It was so nice to be out of doors. She thought perhaps she need not go home just yet. It was so nice to be out in the air. So she would get on to an omnibus. Buses swooped, settled, were off—garish caravans, glistening with red and yellow varnish. But which should she get on to? She had no preferences. She was delighted to be free. The fresh air was so delicious. It had been so stuffy in the Army and Navy Stores. And now it was like riding, to be rushing up Whitehall.

Most flâneurs I encountered in academic literature were men, and, since the term is tied to European traditions of wandering through immigrant and low-income enclaves, I liked the idea of appropriating the method as a woman of color. And as I waded through work from the UCLA and USC scholars who comprised the "L.A. School" of urban geography, I saw that many of them were freeway flâneurs. They'd go in search of wonder, oblivious to the seatbelt holding them back. Noticing this gap gave me the same sense of excitement mixed with fear that I'd felt when perusing bicycle research. If everyone in a field saw things one way, would they welcome a different perspective?

I had tried being a freeway flâneur, long before I would have called it that. I remember as a twenty-year old home on summer break, driving and driving through Orange County and San Diego looking for some spark of magic, some velvet rope I could grasp and pull to tug out into the open a slice of 1960s psychedelia. My college heartbreak had put me on a Pynchonesque quest to find corners where counterculture had survived the Reagan era. I knew the past lay underneath somewhere, or hidden in plain sight. Eventually I drifted outside the car and found my portal to other spacetimes by riding a bicycle. I was also wary of car-based observation because I stopped feeling safe in cars once I started immersing myself in an activist world focused on their dangers, both for the people inside them and outside. Spending so much of my mental energy thinking about the street as a social space weakened my ability to see other road users as inanimate objects around which I could weave. I was turning my life into my research, and in my vulnerable body, I did not see the preference for driving as something neutral. But I did want to find out what motivated other people to stay so strongly attached to it.

In the center of his 1971 book, Banham included a picture of the famous view looking south from the Griffith Observatory in the Hollywood Hills, commenting that, "the great size and lack of distinction of the area covered by this prospect make it the area where Los Angeles is least distinctively itself." The masthead for the blog I started in 2008 called *Urban Adonia* showed the opposite view, staring up at Griffith Park from inside the tallest building seen in Banham's photo, the Equitable Building on Wilshire. Instead of looking down on the Plains of Id from above or through a windshield, I lived down in them. They were my Los Angeles, crusty and surprising and crowded and creative. The vision I had of living at the Ecovillage was that it grappled with the problems of urban living in situ, not segregated in some ecotopian enclave.[26]

---

26 *Ecotopia* is the name of Ernest Callenbach's 1975 book that has been credited with sparking an ecological movement in the Pacific Northwest. Both the book and the environmental movement have been criticized for their blind spots about social inequality. Race problems (people like me) weren't part of the landscape in Ecotopia; as Jeffrey Craig Sanders pointed out in his book *Seattle and the Roots of Urban Sustainability*, "in an era of racial tumult, Callenbach pictured his Ecotopia as a racially divided postapocalyptic society, suggesting a darker side to the new green movement."

It was in that place on purpose because the ecovillagers knew that over and under the stereotype of car-dominated la-la-land there lay a regular old neighborhood where we could take small steps toward healing the collective. L.A.'s sidewalks, corners, and other public spaces were invisible to those who could afford to avoid them, which made them open to a different kind of life.

It felt good to live in a Latino neighborhood again, but I couldn't ignore that the chameleon charm of central L.A.'s public space was starting to get noticed by people who'd been raised to stay out of it. This in-migration was provoking odd juxtapositions like the one I experienced at the vigil on Third Street. I was part of a tide coming in, the part of me that knew about microbrews, Manchego cheese, and cupcake bakeries—the white part of me that had been at home in Portland, the part of me with the bicycle.

Designing CiclAvia in the Shadow of Urban Renewal

5

When the topic of a ciclovía committee came up at the September 2008 LACBC board meeting, it turned out that another guest there, Stephen Villavaso, was also interested in starting something. He was a traffic engineer who had recently moved to L.A. from Austin, Texas. The next day, LACBC's executive director, Jen Klausner, started an email list for people interested in starting a ciclovía in L.A. Bobby and I wrote a report about our visit to Bogotá and speculated as to how a ciclovía might look in Los Angeles. We sent it to the ciclovía list, which had grown to include people beyond LACBC interested in the concept. This was the beginning of two years of organizing it took to hold the first CicLAvia on October 10, 2010.

The committee had its first meeting at Allison Mannos's apartment in East Hollywood on October 28, 2008. Along with Bobby, Stephen, Allison, and me, the organizers from that meeting who stayed on with the effort were environmental policy advocates Jonathan Parfrey and Sandra Hamlat. Jonathan had also seen the ciclovía Streetfilm, and had been circulating it to his networks for some time. He had a long history of work in anti-nuclear and water activism and had much more experience than any of the rest of us in organizing and fundraising. Sandra worked in conservation policy. We were joined at subsequent meetings by Colleen Corcoran, a graphic designer and Stephen's partner.

We met as volunteers on a monthly basis. Our meetings had a non-hierarchical structure. Stephen and Sandra framed it to me as a "meeting of equals," where everyone contributed differently. I took minutes at our meetings, which became valuable field notes for my dissertation project. Our core committee combined people who knew how to navigate the waters of policy and fundraising and people with the technical skills to make the idea seem more possible. Stephen could design a route study that would make sense to engineers with the city; Colleen and her collaborator Joseph Prichard turned our brainstorming into a graphic style. Jonathan suggested creating a visual rendering of what CicLAvia would look like, putting images of bicycles in front of recognizable landmarks, so we put together a promotional presentation combining Bobby's photos from our trip to Bogotá, Stephen's maps, and Colleen's graphics.

The committee was dedicated to including a range of bicycle users in the event by closing streets in low-income central L.A., rather than starting in a more eco-friendly but expensive place like Santa Monica. We discussed routes connecting downtown to Santa Monica, East L.A., the L.A. County Museum of Art near Beverly Hills on Wilshire, and the Hollywood Farmer's Market. When considering names for our imagined event, we weighed the pros and cons of tweaking the unfamiliar term "ciclovía." Maybe it was better to go with something new. Other cities had created new names to describe their events, such as Summer Streets in New York City and Sunday Parkways in Portland. Nine messages into a November 2008 email thread on the ciclovía committee list, Stephen brainstormed, "Via of Ciclovia means a passage or a way thru. The meaning of Ciclovia is of basic elements. How about retaining most of it and call it CicLAvia. When you search CicLAvia, google asks if you meant 'ciclovia.' That could be good." The committee went with Stephen's suggestion, and CicLAvia got its name.

Co-creating CicLAvia became a central component of my graduate fieldwork. Our committee's goal was to make the ciclovía a weekly, city-run program with permanent street signage so that the event would feel open to the public rather than exclusive to those already comfortable with urban bicycling. Through supporting this goal, I pursued two of my own research threads. First, what would it take to turn political will toward something ecologically sound but unpopular? Politicians don't have much incentive to support non-car transportation projects since most of their vocal constituents care a lot about their own car-based commutes. What would make bicycling seem like a transportation option for more people? This first thread explored what the open streets model could do to change public and political attitudes toward sustainable practices like bicycling.

My second research thread had to do with how future streets would be designed, according to whose preferences and values. This was where Jaime's vision of ciclovías in the United States being a decolonizing influence fit in. I knew that urban planning and development had been colonizing tools in Los Angeles during mid-twentieth century urban renewal programs. Now, in an era when city living was becoming the sustainability ideal, who would be defining what changes should be made? How would we undo Autopia in the way streets were designed, maintained, and regulated? And, in undoing Autopia, could we expose and exorcise the fear of racial integration that had made privatized travel so appealing? Through our CicLAvia organizing process, I hypothesized, we could bring a bicycle user's flexible view of streets into top-down city planning. Instead of redeveloping streets, we were advocating for a new street culture.

This distinction between culture change and redevelopment mattered a lot to me. Watching helplessly as open space around my hometown disappeared, I grew up skeptical about profit-driven uses of land. This skepticism took on a new dimension when I learned about the inequitable legacy of federal urban renewal programs in one of my undergraduate anthropology classes. In Los Angeles, as in many cities, development-driven urban renewal wiped whole neighborhoods off the map. I was drawn in particular to the erasure of Bunker Hill downtown. Early filmstrips of Bunker Hill show Victorian mansions lining the slopes on each side of the Angel's Flight funicular train, displaying the opulence of the neighborhood at the end of the nineteenth century. By the 1930s, wealthy families had moved on from downtown mansions to more fashionable addresses, and the neighborhood became a tenement district. The mansions were subdivided into multiple apartments to accommodate migrant laborers, the elderly, and the indigent.

I found relics of Bunker Hill in the works of the writer John Fante and the filmmaker Kent MacKenzie. While living in Bunker Hill in the 1930s, Fante wrote stories about his struggle to succeed as a writer, describing a hardscrabble life in a city center full of rooming houses. His 1939 novel *Ask the Dust* is his most well known book and to me it captures the restless fumbling to catch truth in words that can drive writers mad. Fante's characters, mostly autobiographical sketches based on his own Italian-American family, fall hard for Mexican-American waitresses in diners and bum around amidst the immigrants and invalids. In his stories, Fante used downtown L.A. as a backdrop to heighten his own desperation. As the neighborhood decayed, Bunker Hill similarly became the setting of many noir stories in print and on film, where it played the role of seedy urban jungle.

Kent MacKenzie's 1961 film *The Exiles* did something different, instead portraying Bunker Hill through the eyes of Native American actors. Presented in a photojournalistic style, MacKenzie's cameras followed a young woman, portrayed by Yvonne Williams, on her evening wandering through the bustling streets of downtown L.A., to her home in the quieter Bunker Hill district. The viewer watches as this young woman sits in one of the ornate movie houses on Broadway, giant white faces stretched out on the screen above her. While the film is flawed by today's standards (when I've shown *The Exiles* to students they've expressed discomfort with its stereotypic portrayal of Indians and alcohol), it's the only one I've seen from its era that puts those living in L.A. blight at the center of its narrative.

By the 1950s, the entire Bunker Hill neighborhood was slated for federally funded demolition as a blighted zone. The Community Redevelopment Agency promised residents that affordable housing would be built to replace the deteriorating houses once they cleared the hill to make way for private investment. Fighting against their depiction of Bunker Hill as an unsanitary breeding ground for vice, MacKenzie made another film that showed a different vision of the neighborhood. *Bunker Hill – 1956* interviewed elderly white residents who spoke about their daily lives at home or visiting nearby businesses. The Bunker Hill of *The Exiles* has no place in this earlier film, perhaps because its Native and Mexican protagonists did not help market the neighborhood as a perfectly decent white space. Despite this whitewashing, the advocates for Bunker Hill failed. The Victorian mansions that once covered its steep slopes have gone, replaced by glass and steel towers, or by nothing at all. Most of the housing was not replaced, so the district ceased to be a residential one for the most part.

It was a destructive era of urban planning, even for those who escaped displacement. Urban planner Kevin Lynch, in his 1960 study *The Image of the City*, documented how disoriented L.A. residents felt in the new landscape that resulted from urban renewal's massive changes to the built environment. For those in its crosshairs, it was much worse. Above downtown Los Angeles, near Elysian Park, Chávez Ravine offers an infamous tale about the profound misuse of federal redevelopment funds to destroy a community. Don Normark's book *Chávez Ravine: A Los Angeles Story* details how efforts to clear the land for an ambitious public housing development began in the early 1950s, when the families who lived in the ravine's three barrios were evicted and given paltry sums for relocation.[27]

The project was the brainchild of Frank Wilkinson, an idealistic planner with the city housing authority. He'd worked with architect Richard Neutra to design a much more dense neighborhood plan for the site. The displaced residents themselves had not been part of this planning process, though they were supposed to be able to move back in after their homes had been bulldozed and replaced. However, with the election of a new mayor unfriendly to public housing, Wilkinson was accused of being a communist and ended up in jail. Meanwhile, the housing project was canceled and the city sold the cleared land to the owner of the Brooklyn Dodgers, Walter O'Malley, who supposedly had seen Chávez Ravine from the air and decided it would be a good site for the city's proposed stadium.

In images from a Los Angeles Public Library collection, I found a graphic memory of the final chapter. A 1959 picture shows a brown woman, Aurora Vargas, with her hair arranged carefully in the style of the day. She's barefoot and police are pulling her away from her home. Her face is angry; she seems to be shouting. Behind her a little girl cries, frightened at the spectacle before her. Aurora is twisting to escape the policemen's grip. Soon afterwards, her neighborhood was buried under concrete. Another picture in the collection is titled "Draftsmen through, bring on the shovels," and shows a white man in a suit pointing to a plan of the stadium standing on an easel. He's got several chins and round glasses,

---

27 Another good resource for the story of Chávez Ravine is Jordan Mechner's 2004 documentary about the neighborhood and its inhabitants.

and he smiles as he holds up a commemorative shovel marking September 17, 1959 as the day stadium construction began.

These stories abound all over the U.S., and they are still living in the memories of the families who experienced them. Urban centers like L.A.'s may have gone through decades of being unfashionable, but they are not blank slates. What seemed genius to me about bringing the ciclovía to L.A. was that it would show who was already there on our streets. I hoped it could be a way to the future through the diverse present, and making it an official event seemed like it would put city power behind a participatory model. At our November 2008 meeting, we discussed seeking then-city councilmember Eric Garcetti's support. Garcetti's council district encompassed several of the central neighborhoods we wanted our first route to pass through, including East Hollywood and the Ecovillage's edge of K-Town. Sandra reached out to her friend Romel Pascual, a deputy to Mayor Antonio Villaraigosa, and other insiders about our idea.

In part because of urban renewal's completely uneven distribution of benefits and burdens, "community engagement" requirements had been built into the official street change process. Advocates around the country were working in this planning process to undo the mistakes of urban renewal. New urbanist media in particular focused on car-based planning as wrong, and "human-scale" planning as the way to go. Keeping in mind the need to appeal to people beyond self-identified cycling enthusiasts, we created messaging about our event creating a temporary park space as a response to Los Angeles' "park poor" status. Viewing streets as living public spaces had growing cachet, as seen in the popularity of Park(ing) Day, which started in San Francisco in 2005. Park(ing) Day, which had also taken hold in L.A., encouraged individuals and groups to feed parking meters in order to use the spaces not for holding cars, but to create temporary social spaces. Astroturf and lawn chairs were popular, and people brought out potted plants and held picnics in the street. It was an open street event that did not require a city permit.

At our next meeting in December, we discussed how to bring more activists into the effort. When we got in touch with other U.S. cities holding ciclovías, such as Portland, Chicago, New York, and Miami, we learned that we were the only city in the United States to start with a grassroots ciclovía campaign. All other cities' events came from public employees who thought it sounded like a good idea, perhaps after witnessing one of the charismatic Peñalosas in action. Because we did not have the city's support yet, we needed to find supporters along our proposed route. We should always, Jonathan cautioned, be respectful of groups who see themselves as gatekeepers. For the MacArthur Park area, for example, we should reach out to immigration advocacy groups. Jonathan emphasized that many people were becoming aware of bicycle and pedestrian infrastructure issues: transportation people, parks people, and even economic forecasters.

The route scouting we did kept us grounded in our vision for the event, which could get bogged down in the logistical planning we did at our meetings around event insurance, political support, and fundraising, whether to plan our own event without city support, whether to try to take over a "name" street like Sunset or Wilshire. For one route-scouting ride, Bobby, Stephen, Colleen, Sandra, and I met at MacArthur Park and biked west on Wilshire Boulevard as far as the L.A. County Museum of Art. Stephen and I took notes on sites that might be negatively impacted by a Sunday street closure, such as churches with parking lots that only opened onto Wilshire, and potential allies, such as cultural organizations. We scanned each block and thought about ways an eco-friendly dry cleaner, or a Korean radio station, or an empty park space at the base of a large corporate plaza, might be transformed by crowds of bicyclists. Through our eyes, this heavily congested, car-dominated stretch of Los Angeles became a riverbed where we could see a flood of people biking and walking. A flood that would grow from the steady trickle of people already biking and walking on the sidewalks of Wilshire.

In creating a space for both captive bicycle users and carfree ones, I wanted to provoke dialogue on the wiggle room between official infrastructure and everyday street life, which I was studying in grad school. Anthropologists are trained to observe what the French geographer Henri Lefebvre called the "production of space." We don't take it for granted that people are living in accordance with the intentions of planners and designers; instead, we look for the gaps between formal and informal systems. I learned that this was not as common in urban planning, the field tasked with building and maintaining our shared environments. The planning system treats informality primarily as a nuisance, something to be regulated or eliminated. Anthropologists are less interested in formal order than we are in why people develop informal systems and the nature of those systems. We spend years of fieldwork observing that marginalized people often figure out how to survive despite the plans of people more powerful than them. As an urban anthropologist, I wondered what kind of planning solutions could come from these informal systems. From this perspective, an intervention like CicLAvia could root street planning in the realities of people who didn't see themselves as urbanists or designers.

In December 2008, I encountered someone who was already articulating this approach to street planning. Chicano artist and urban planner James Rojas believed that everyone had valuable knowledge about urban design. In examining how Latinx immigrants made themselves at home in L.A. neighborhoods built by white settlers in the early 1900s, James highlighted the flexibility of public and private space. From his perspective, places expressed cultural identity, and if we took this as a given, it become very clear that what made a place "good" or "bad" was intricately tied up with racialized and classed notions of whose culture mattered. This was exactly the kind of reflection on and rejection of racial-cultural discrimination that I hoped CicLAvia would provoke along its route.

I met James when I was tabling for the Ecovillage at a Natural History Museum sustainability event. Across the hall stood a short man with a distinctive coif, next to a table covered in plastic figurines and tiny, Lego-style objects. The toys sat on a map of Los Angeles. Children and adults hung around the table, moving pieces around. James used model building as a technique to encourage people to be creative with their city, bringing urban planning down to the scale of individual hands. Planning jargon was less accessible than our sensory memories of place. Later that day, I listened to him give a lecture about Latinos and sustainable practices in East L.A. where he had grown up. Back in the 90s, he'd written a master's thesis at MIT on East L.A.'s "enacted environment," and now he was an urban planner at Metro. James showed pictures of businesses where shopkeepers had turned sidewalks into displays of their wares, private yards filled with Catholic icons and folkloric collections, and garages that had been converted into living spaces. He spoke enthusiastically about how immigrant families were ingeniously adding density to neighborhoods composed of single-family homes with these garage conversions.

James mentioned that the rates of bike fatalities in L.A. County were highest among Latino males between the ages of 30 and 40, and that these men were often on their way to or from work. Afterwards, I asked him if the people he spoke with ever used the terms "sustainable" or "green." He said that they did not. Bike users like the men James mentioned, and others who practiced "green" lifestyles out of poverty, had less access to political capital than people like James and me. We were Chicanxs who, in observing and participating in L.A. urban sustainability, thought across these realms. Maybe we could be a bridge because we saw the beauty in "rascuache," the Chicanx term for DIY that is both functional and aesthetic. Think of using a coffee tin as a flowerpot, or other inventive ways of recycling materials. Plenty of Chicanxs strive for more readymade ways of living, but some of us are at home in the slippage between design and making do. Maybe this was why the bicycle appealed to me as a research object and tool; as Alfredo Mirandé and Raymond L. Williams have pointed out, it is a rascuache machine.[28]

The reason I think that the shared identity mattered was that unlike many other architects, artists, and urban planners whose work I have encountered, James did not leave the people doing the creative things he admired out of the picture. In his push to include Latino everyday practices in the scope of urbanism, he sought to use his expert status to expand the paradigm of urban planning. What James and others call "Latinx urbanism" doesn't have to do with using the city right or wrong; it acknowledges how our engagement with the material world emerges through our mestizaje and our migration. We carry the borderlands inside of us and express them in our neighborhoods. As Victor Valle and Rodolfo Torres argued in their 2000 book *Latino Metropolis*, this creativity should be seen as a major contributor to the character of U.S. urbanism, especially in the southwest. People like James wanted to incorporate into the urban planning process that Latinxs redesign existing built environments through their cultural practices.

---

28 I'm referring to "Rascuache Cycling Justice," Mirandé and Williams' chapter in the 2016 book I co-edited, *Bicycle Justice and Urban Transformation*.

We held a ciclovía workshop at James' gallery downtown, g727, in June 2009. He asked participants to design bike-friendly spaces for CicLAvia, everyone at their own placemat. One attendee was a Colombian-Puerto Rican artist named Carolina Caycedo who had a show up in the gallery. She spoke enthusiastically about growing up with Bogotá's ciclovía, and talked about the lively social space it gave to teens for flirting and preening. Carolina's interactive art show, "DAYTODAY" (2009), centered on a seven-year long experiment where she sought to tie different people together through things they offered each other. She circulated a flyer listing what she could offer and what she sought, putting the focus on exchange as the art practice. I envisioned CicLAvia as a connection space along these lines, a break from how traffic infrastructure limits our acknowledgement of each other. CicLAvia had been designed to reveal the flexibility of the built environment, and how those around us contributed to our sense of place. This would lead to a rejection of street contempt, and a channeling of public funding for transportation into local programs that repaired social relationships. Urban renewal was over, the enacted street was here.

Meanwhile, Bunker Hill's remaining dirt lots were dwindling, covered over by celebrated starchitecture anchoring the power brokers' old, old dreams of a world-class downtown. And finally, white money was coming back into the city. We were on the brink of major change, again. Could CicLAvia help things go better this time around?

Sacred and Profane Street Life

6

By the end of 2008, I had embarked on two fieldwork projects that aimed to expand public participation in riding bikes and planning streets. At the same time that CicLAvia was taking shape, I was brainstorming with a different group about how we could make bike advocacy into a vehicle for more bicycle users' perspectives. It started rolling when I met Allison Mannos, a CicLAvia collaborator. She wore a neckerchief and an asymmetrical hairstyle, and she was fired up about using urban planning as a social justice tool. Allison grew up in the L.A. suburbs and like me she had mixed roots. Her ancestors were Jewish and Chinese immigrants. Hearing her talk about being mixed race made me consider that I had something in common with mixed people beyond the white and Mexican sides of my own background. Allison was a student at UCLA and had just started an internship at LACBC.

We both noticed that certain L.A. cyclists were riding under the radar of the organized bike movement, and Allison introduced me to others she'd been talking with about the issue: Dorothy Le, her colleague at LACBC, and Andy Rodriguez, her friend. Allison named our fledgling collaboration City of Lights/Ciudad de Luces because our first plan was to distribute bike lights, and because we wanted to shed some light on bicycling undertaken by Spanish-speaking workers. As we started writing funding proposals for City of Lights, Allison told me about a 2005 report LACBC had written for Metro that investigated the needs and habits of existing bicyclists in Los Angeles County. As stated in the report, "the purpose . . . was to gain a better understanding of the needs and perceptions of the broadest possible range of bicyclists with a particular emphasis on those in low-income, transit-dependent communities." To accomplish this, they used a team of bilingual individuals who administered surveys to bicyclists all over the county.

The report described low-income, Latino men who rode bicycles as "invisible," as did an article L.A. writer Dan Koeppel published in the December 2005 issue of *Bicycling* magazine. Koeppel's piece focused on riders for whom using a bicycle was a necessary evil rather than a fun choice. Visible and invisible were loaded terms in bicycle advocacy, where street safety was a central topic and there was a big emphasis on being seen. Groups around the country produced PSAs focused on eye contact and campaigns distributed tools for increasing visibility. It seemed like the "invisible riders" term pointed to something beyond the dangers of being overlooked by motorists: these bike users had been left out of organized efforts to influence public policy and street design. However, it wasn't clear that naming the problem had led to action.

The 2005 LACBC report acknowledged a need for outreach, and had been designed to gather surveys on cyclist preferences and habits at transit stations, worker centers, and other strategic locations in order to learn about what its authors termed "traditionally hard-to-reach and underrepresented bicyclists." The report included calls to "promote and fund culturally-sensitive vehicular bicycling and safety programs in low-income communities" and to "promote and fund programs that make helmet, lights and reflective clothing available in low-income communities."[29] As of 2008, no measures had been taken to

29 The assumption made in this report, one that I did not question at the time, was that the bike

address the recommendations in the report. That changed when Allison started her internship at LACBC.

The City of Lights team started planning how to use bike light giveaways as an opportunity to meet Latino bicycle users in the central L.A. neighborhoods where we lived. Our goal was to connect different kinds of bike users to advocacy. We would increase public participation in street planning by getting to know the people obscured by the term invisible rider.[30] In bringing a different set of concerns to the attention of city officials and planners, we wanted to follow the transit justice move to address the exclusion of racialized communities from the policy process and public investment.

It was definitely easier to identify gaps in movement networks than it was to close them. For example, in October 2009, I biked with friends to a library in South L.A. to attend one of the city's bike master plan update meetings. Creating bicycle master plans allows cities to access federal transportation funding to build more bike-specific facilities. The usual crowd of bike advocates milled around, talking to Department of Transportation staff and planners from the firm hired to manage the update, Alta Planning + Design. We were encouraged to draw on maps, make comments on plan language, and submit comment cards. Few people made comments on the portion of the map representing the historically black and more recently Latino neighborhood we were standing in, presumably because most of us lived in other parts of the city.

movement's lack of knowledge about bike resources in low-income neighborhoods meant that there were none. I came to see this as incorrect, partially through my own research but mainly through the work of journalist Sahra Sulaiman, who has written for online magazine *Los Angeles Streetsblog* since 2012 and brings to light complex realities from South Central L.A. streets.

30 I find the term "core riders" to be more appropriate than invisible riders. The term was introduced to me by Stephanie Pollack, a public transit researcher and advocate who became the Secretary of Transportation for the State of Massachusetts in 2015. Pollack defined the term as the lead author of reports such as "Maintaining Diversity in America's Transit-Rich Neighborhoods" published in 2010 by the Dukakis Center for Urban and Regional Policy at Northeastern University.

Outside the window, I saw several people of color biking down the sidewalks of busy Western Avenue. The meeting seemed like a response to bike advocates' view that we were an embattled minority neglected by the city, but it clearly wasn't reaching the people I saw biking outside.

It seemed likely that some bicycle users felt safer staying hidden, and I knew how much work went into being invisible. Mixed-race people like me develop complex strategies for minimizing our differences when we need to, appearing nonchalant while drawing on a sophisticated understanding of the systems designed without us in mind. Obviously staying out of sight was important for Los Angeles' population of people living undocumented, and working on City of Lights showed me how bicycling was just another survival strategy. This meant that instead of responding to their mobile marginality by lobbying local government the way bicycle advocates did, these core riders "[sought] to remain invisible to the gaze of the city's regulating mechanisms," as planning scholar Gerardo Sandoval characterized the goal of people living *sin papeles*.[31]

The bike infrastructure strategy had been designed to fit the urban planning process, which made it a poor fit for those under pressure to keep out of sight. Planning for bicycle transportation mostly didn't happen unless there was a self-identified bike group lobbying for it, and bike advocates I knew tended to present their case in as technical a format as possible. What they knew from riding bicycles had to be presented as objective knowledge, based, if possible, on some "best practice" model circulating among bicycle and pedestrian planning professionals online. LACBC had active projects piloting a bicyclist and pedestrian count that would quantify non-motorized users, and a sharrows

31 The quote is from Sandoval's 2010 book *Immigrants and the Revitalization of Los Angeles: Development and Change in MacArthur Park.*

project funded by Councilmember Garcetti's office that would quantify the effectiveness of a bike symbol on a street. Neither project involved working closely with bicycle users that they would not already know through their social networks. They'd rely on street intercept surveys to gather public opinions outside those networks rather than more in-depth community outreach. Speaking as community members, but wielding the language of planning, bike advocates were trying to set their own preferences in stone, so to speak.

The problem with this was that bicycling encompassed a pretty wide variety of people, places, and things. Each person brings a particular body to a particular environment on a particular machine, so no two rides are completely alike. Lights change, other people on the road bring good and bad moods, you get a flat tire or glide along. Our feelings of safety are tied to what we know from past experience, what we have heard about a place, what our parents impressed upon us as we walked out the door. In short, riding a bicycle is deeply perspectival.

When scholars talk about "perspective," we mean that each of us views the world through a very personalized lens crafted by our memories and our cultural values. For feminist theorists like Donna Haraway, acknowledging our own perspectives can be a way to fight oppression, countering the "view from nowhere" that those dominant within our culture use to claim that their own perspectives are objective. Riding a bicycle had given me more of a sense of physical power than I'd ever had; and not just physical, I felt like I could change the world. Flattening the diversity of bicycle users into quantitative measures didn't sit right with me, but the political world of public spending required compressing the complexity of real life into a cardboard cutout. More and more it seemed like bike advocates expected so-called invisible riders to make themselves fit into chosen strategies, while with City of

Lights we were trying to go back to the drawing board and develop strategies responsive to a broader group.

City of Lights did not have many peers at the time we started organizing, but there was one group, coincidentally named City Lites, that had been making the connection between bikes and empowerment in the black community for some years. I learned about City Lites in early 2009 through helping to plan the L.A. Bike Summit. In late 2008, Bob Gottlieb, then the director of Occidental College's Urban & Environmental Policy Institute, started working with Joe Linton to plan a one-day conference that would bring together people involved in various bike projects around the county.[32] City Lites' organizers had submitted a workshop proposal discussing their annual bike event in South L.A., so to learn more I arranged to sit in at their planning meeting in January 2009.

As I got off the bus in the early winter night, I noted that unlike my bustling neighborhood 80 blocks up Vermont Avenue, this part of town had little foot traffic. The planning meeting was led by a black man named Mark Johnson, and the meeting's attendees ran through the logistics for putting on the Inner City Sports Event, a children's bicycle festival in Jesse Owens Park in the nearby Hawthorne neighborhood. There did not seem to be much interest in bicycling itself at the meeting, but rather how bicycles could be tools to engage youth around health and safety. Someone said that the festival was an opportunity to "show folks our community is not like you think it is." Another committee

---

32 Gottlieb had been instrumental in the production of ArroyoFest, a bike and pedestrian event that had closed down the 110 Freeway in Pasadena for a day in 2003. Gottlieb chronicled its planning and the excitement of the day in a book, *Reinventing Los Angeles*. ArroyoFest meant to remind people that the 110 had been designed, as the Arroyo Seco Parkway, "to establish a visual connection to the surrounding landscape and communities and partly as a modern freeway that would significantly improve the speed in which drivers could arrive at their destination." Though it only happened once, ArroyoFest made enough of an impact on the urban design milieu in L.A. that I heard about it a number of times while working on CicLAvia.

member explained that, historically, biking was not an option in these neighborhoods because of gang issues. Training for the bike tour would bring families together around health and fitness. This vision for bicycling's role was new to me, different from the political advocacy focus up in central L.A. The Inner City Sports Event, focused on a park, enlisted bicycles in the fight for community safety and family health rather than transforming street design.

The Bike Summit took place in early March 2009 at L.A. Trade Technical College on the south end of downtown. Most of the bike activists I'd met over the last six months attended to hear guest speakers from Mexico City and Portland and to participate in workshops about bike issues in L.A. I attended the City Lites presentation, and was surprised to see Mark Johnson seem awkward in this setting in comparison with his command at his own meeting. There, organizers stopped during the meeting to commend each other's work on the project. The group camaraderie was palpable. But here, presenting to bike advocates and transportation professionals, he seemed out of his element. When an LACBC board member asked what his organization needed from the bike movement, Johnson did not push for collaboration. It seemed that programs with a community focus didn't fit neatly into a bike advocacy paradigm focused on infrastructure.

My own collaboration, City of Lights, certainly didn't have readymade solutions for transforming bike advocacy; we were still trying to figure out how to connect respectfully with our target population. It was going to take a while to find out how we could even be of service to the most vulnerable bicycle users. City of Lights' first action was to distribute lights and safety information to volunteers who would hand them out on street corners, but these interactions were fleeting and we felt like we were racially profiling bike users. We needed a different approach. In April 2009, Allison and I met with staffer Jose Velíz at a worker center near MacArthur Park operated by CARECEN, the Central American Resource Center. He invited us to use their facility as a staging ground for light distribution, safety workshops, and general bike education and community building activities. CARECEN's worker center sat on the edge of a Home Depot parking lot and consisted of an open-air hall enclosed by fences, with office space at each end. Usually, somebody was teaching an English class while *jornaleros* (day laborers) sat on folding chairs, paying more or less attention, sipping coffee, waiting for work. Many people using the center had bikes locked up to the fence and trees outside.

We started spending a few hours there every Friday, installing lights and chatting with jornalero cyclists. Everyone on the City of Lights team spoke Spanish, with varying degrees of fluency. We made quite a spectacle, as a group mostly composed of young women, in a space filled with men looking for ways to pass their unpaid time. We would set up a table in an alcove facing the sidewalk outside the fence, hang a banner, and install lights. Men lined up with their bikes and we installed lights with our multi-tools.

While I spoke my belabored Spanish and struggled to concentrate on installing the plastic light housing on myriad handlebars, I felt many men's eyes on me. It took me back to when I was a growing girl child who, in a Mexican neighborhood, attracted approving looks and sounds from men relaxing on stoops as I walked past. By age thirteen, I had learned to look straight ahead and avoid eye contact. Wooden, chaste, free. I only knew how to be alone in Latino public space, where women are supposed to guard their modesty against a constant male gaze. I had not anticipated this gendered conditioning coming up in my dissertation research and activism, but being chatty and charming, the style I use as an ethnographer, made me feel vulnerable in a context where that kind of behavior could come across as flirtatious.

In an essay on ethnography and infrastructure, the anthropologist Susan Leigh Star wrote that "surfacing invisible work" was an important reason why we should spend time witnessing the everyday life of infrastructure systems.[33] In studying streets and trying to push past the dismissal of invisible riders, I had unexpectedly uncovered my own gendered work to stay disengaged in Latino public space. Nobody at the CARECEN site harassed me, but I felt conflicted. As a PhD. researcher and citizen at home in white culture, I had access to privileges that gave me far more power than the jornaleros I was meeting; something felt off about gaining the trust of individuals who, while we lived close to each other, inhabited a different world than I did. I didn't know who to ask for advice about what I would now call my experience of intersectionality. I had wanted to blow up the idea of the invisible cyclist by learning the in-depth life stories of the people dehumanized by that term, but in the end, I didn't know how to use City of Lights ethnographically.

However, I still learned why so many Latino bicycle users chose to ride on sidewalks rather than in traffic. For some, the sidewalks of L.A. represented a vast improvement over biking on streets with no sidewalks at all. One man told me that biking here was much better than biking in Guatemala City. Others wished to avoid attracting police attention. In some cases, we could see why they avoided riding in traffic as soon as we looked at their bikes. One person had been riding without his seat post locked into place, others rode on tires without tubes inside them, and many had

---

33 Star's 1999 essay, "The Ethnography of Infrastructure," was published in *American Behavioral Scientist*.

bikes that did not fit them comfortably. Riding slowly on sidewalks made commuting on these broken machines possible. Some of the people we talked to said they chose not to bring their bikes to the center because if they got work and had to leave the bike all day, it might not be there when they returned. Often we had to remove some older plastic mounting device from handlebars, a remnant of a light the owner had lost to theft.

Sidewalk riding wasn't always an effective strategy for staying invisible, since police officers had the authority to interpret legal codes and sometimes chose to target sidewalk riders. We heard about cases like this at CARECEN, and we also heard that police sometimes wrote tickets to immigrant cyclists for not wearing helmets, even though L.A. did not have a mandatory helmet law for adults. Traffic tickets are an economic burden that can push low-income people into debt, and for those living undocumented, the consequences can be dire. Talking to jornaleros made it clear that pursuing better streets through law enforcement did not increase safety for all.

One opportunity for racial profiling in policing was an ambiguous city ordinance that prohibited riding bicycles on sidewalks with a wanton or willful disregard for pedestrian safety, so City of Lights decided to ask Los Angeles Police Department directly about the issue. We thought maybe we could learn their internal practice around when to enforce the ordinance and share this with jornaleros. In early September 2009, Allison and Andy set up a meeting with LAPD, and two instructors who trained bike cops met us at LACBC's office. They told us that thousands of officers had been through their training, though only about 150 were on duty using bikes at any given time. When we posed the sidewalk-riding question, the instructors said they could not influence police officer behavior because cops would not listen to guidance from people not working a beat. Each police officer interpreted the ordinance in question at his/her own discretion. Because of this need for officer discretion, they said, we would be better off asking city council for changes in signage and regulations than asking LAPD for changes in enforcement.

Another recent issue had been police officers ticketing people for biking in crosswalks. We asked the LAPD bike instructors about this, and listened as they explained that a person walking a bicycle is a pedestrian, while a person riding a bicycle is a vehicle. Using a vehicle in a crosswalk is illegal, and bicyclists who rode in crosswalks could also be cited for traveling against traffic. Bicyclists occupy a legal gray zone, being classified alternately as vehicles and as pedestrians. However, the instructors didn't explain why officers would choose to target this form of mobility when there was plenty of lawbreaking coming from people driving much more dangerous vehicles. There was no consideration of the vulnerability that led to people choosing to ride on sidewalks in the first place, as though aggressive motorist behavior had nothing to do with bicyclist behavior. To me it seemed absurd to cite a man riding a bicycle down a busy street with an empty sidewalk because he did not dismount to walk his bike across an empty crosswalk. Bicyclists were subject to the same traffic pressures as motorists, but because we stuck out more, we might be subject to more discretionary police enforcement than motorists. No wonder people wanted to fly under the radar and seek the privacy of cars.

I felt a growing sense of futility as the meeting wore on. I had experienced the frustration of discretionary enforcement as a pedestrian myself. On our way to a CicLAvia meeting in March 2009, Bobby and I were crossing Vermont at Third Street. The light was green, but the crosswalk signal, the kind that had numbers counting down as the red hand flashed, had already started flashing red. The light was still green when we reached the other side of the street, when a police officer on a motorcycle roared up next to us on the sidewalk and stopped us short. He also stopped a Latina woman pushing a laundry cart and proceeded to write us all jaywalking tickets. Our technical error had been in entering the street after the red hand had started flashing, we were told. We were fined 170 dollars each. As he wrote out the tickets, I watched motorists passing into the intersection after the light had turned red, a common practice at that intersection and all over Los Angeles.

Bobby and I were street activists on our way to a room full of sympathetic ears. We didn't want to pay the fine, but it wouldn't put us in debt. I felt angry on behalf of the woman with the laundry cart. I don't know what that ticket set into motion for her. And all of this ostensibly was to keep us safe. It reminded me of the ubiquitous LAPD helicopters that made it hard to sleep on an almost nightly basis, whose thud-thud-thud made me want to cower like a child, not from some unseen threat, but from the very visible and audible demonstration of state-sanctioned force.

At our next City of Lights meeting a few days after the LAPD meeting, we made plans to stake out a spot near MacArthur Park for the upcoming Park(ing) Day, the public space event where people feed parking meters and set up mini-parks in the street. It proved to be a disappointment. First we set up a canopy to protect us from L.A.'s blazing September heat in a parking space at the northwest corner of Wilshire Boulevard as it crossed MacArthur Park. We laid out information about City of Lights, hung our banner, put on rock en español, and got ready to make a spectacle of ourselves reclaiming space from cars. We quickly attracted attention, but not the kind we had hoped. Two police officers stopped next to us and told us to get out of the street. They said that we could not put up a canopy in the street. Ok, we said, we can take it down. No, they said, you cannot be in the street. I spent a few minutes trying to explain to the officers that this event was taking place all over town, with other sites to be found a short distance west on Wilshire, and that it seemed discriminatory to say it could not happen in MacArthur Park. They did not budge; our brown bodies simply were not allowed to reinvent the street. Arguing with the police officers didn't get me anywhere but mad.

After we gave up, I biked down to those other sites further west on Wilshire where a whiter and more affluent crowd was enjoying astroturf and beach chairs in parking spaces. I tried to explain my frustration to friends there, but the music playing and picnic vibe drowned it out. Today this sort of intervention is called "tactical urbanism," and I tend to be wary when I hear about it because of that day in September 2009. Street interventions aren't magic; it's *who* is interested in playing in the street that makes street furniture and "reclaiming" space legitimate. It occurred to me that I was witnessing a latter-day version of what Carey McWilliams called the sacred/profane split, the vilification of certain bodies and simultaneous uplift of the landscapes they'd inhabited.

Bringing Park(ing) Day to MacArthur Park was supposed to be a symbolic statement about the inclusion of all Angelenos in the city's sustainable future. Instead, it became a reaffirmation that bodies in the street get policed differently. The police were not likely to help us bridge between informal survival and the idealistic urban transformation some of us had in mind. Liberating the streets would not be an equitable design project if we didn't also address the unequal treatment faced by the people who used them.

Human Infrastructure

My life was such a whirlwind of activity from 2008 to 2010 that I did not bring my concern about the sacred places/profane people split into the design of CicLAvia. I didn't question whether our goal of becoming a city-sponsored event could limit CicLAvia to the realm of what was politically palatable, thereby neutralizing its potential to be a space of resistance. I was learning for the first time about the human infrastructure that activists, officials, and city staff comprise as they turn private priorities into public ones; I wasn't sophisticated enough to recognize the compromises that come with the territory. I believed very strongly in CicLAvia's potential to disrupt car culture and I assumed the decolonizing effect I envisioned would be a major part of the event's ongoing life in L.A. This belief gave me the energy for organizing work almost every evening at a time when I was also commuting by train and bike to my university campus 47 miles south of Los Angeles, spending four hours a day in transit at least three times a week.

By the spring of 2009, our organizing committee was building momentum. Joe Linton joined the CicLAvia committee after seeing our presentation at the Bike Summit in March 2009. He became a core organizer of the event and brought in a tremendous amount of knowledge about transportation policy in L.A., something we had been lacking. Then, in May 2009, Lois at the Ecovillage directed me to a new issue of *Los Angeles Magazine* where figures in different fields had been asked how they would advise the mayor on L.A.'s future. One person, Aaron Paley of an art events company called Community Arts Resources (CARS), suggested a ciclovía. I emailed him and told him about CicLAvia, and he responded enthusiastically. Aaron was headed to Bogotá that month, so I also sent an email connecting him with Jaime Ortiz. By July, the CicLAvia committee was meeting at CARS' offices in the Wiltern Building at Wilshire and Western. As an experienced event planner, Aaron helped the committee focus our efforts on political support and fundraising.

We secured Mayor Antonio Villaraigosa's tentative endorsement that fall, but political will shifted further in our favor in December 2009. Mayor Villaraigosa attended the United Nations Climate Change Summit in Copenhagen, which brought politicians from all over the world to what bike advocates consider the model city for bike infrastructure. While there, a radio show interviewed him, and the host asked him what plans L.A. had to promote bicycling. Villaraigosa alluded to a street closure event that was in the works. Even though he did not mention our effort by name, this was a big deal because it was the first time he had publicly acknowledged his support for CicLAvia. This meant we could represent our future event to potential funders as city-sanctioned.

In January 2010 we started meeting with city staff to plan the logistics of our first event, which would allow us to get a firm estimate of how much the event would cost. At this point, our proposed route included thirteen miles of streets. Things moved slowly because staff from the Los Angeles Department of Transportation (LADOT) and the Bureau of Street Services were uninterested and skeptical. Even though we had the mayor's support, these bureaucrats had their reasons for resisting working with us. In one meeting, a supervisor from LADOT told us that, "the streets were made for parking and travel. They weren't made for an event." Several times, staff mentioned a horrific incident in which an elderly man drove a car into a pedestrianized space in Santa Monica and did not brake before killing multiple people.

More recently, a motorist had driven onto the closed route of a triathlon and struck a participant, leaving him paralyzed. The victim sued the city and won significant damages. The rumor was that this exercise in liability cost the city millions and made them adamant that we must have at least six traffic safety officers at each intersection where traffic would cross the route. Paying off-duty officers overtime wages would make our event much more expensive than we had anticipated, and this was one reason why the event got cut down from 13 to seven-and-a-half miles.

Another reason was that the city staff responsible for estimating the costs of the street closure did not want to provide an estimate for the full route we initially proposed. Citing limited work hours, the city worker assigned to help us with logistics said he could only cost a seven-and-a-half mile route. Later an LADOT traffic engineer rejected a section of the proposed route that would divert motorists from a surface street onto a highway, informing us that, "we don't force people to get on the freeways. Some people don't feel comfortable driving on the freeway." The message was that LADOT recognized that people might fear driving, but was not responsible for providing alternative travel options. Negotiating with the city further proved the need for an event that gave people the opportunity to feel comfortable outside of their cars on city streets. It also highlighted to me how little our sustainable transportation movements had infiltrated the suburb-dwelling, car-driving culture that was the norm within government agencies. Working for government has long been seen as a pathway to the middle class, and in meeting after meeting I saw it reinforced that these professionals did not see what we were planning as something for them or their families.

Through the spring of 2010, even as we were meeting with city staff to plan logistics for the event, the mayor's office lagged in giving us an official letter of support that we could take to funders, or to guarantee that they would pay for half of the event's expenses. As the months wore on and we started sharing our October 10 target date with the public, we remained apprehensive that the city would renege and leave us with an event we could not fund. But then the mayor crashed his bike, and we learned how transformative institutional power can be when bodily experience intervenes.

Villaraigosa sometimes engaged in the high-status pastime of recreational cycling, taking long rides through L.A. on weekends. On one such ride, he was traveling in a bike lane on high-speed, congested Venice Boulevard when a motorist pulled out in front of him. Startled, Villaraigosa crashed his bike and ended up injured. When the news broke, the L.A. bike movement stood up and shouted a collective "I told you so!" regarding the city's poor biking conditions. In response, Villaraigosa had his aides plan a mayor's bike summit where all of us could come to the Metro headquarters and air our grievances for 90 seconds apiece. Word spread among the bike community through blogs, meetings, and flyers. The mayor's bodily entanglements in Copenhagen and on Venice Boulevard became significant milestones for CicLAvia. We were really going to make this thing happen.

Once we had the mayor's support, Villaraigosa put the CicLAvia committee to work. We were invited to speak at the mayor's bike summit, and Aaron and I showed up armed with t-shirts and a quick presentation. Many people in the room already knew about CicLAvia. "I was already supporting this event before the accident," the mayor assured the standing-room only audience, crammed in with their messenger bags and helmets. In that moment, CicLAvia provided the evidence he needed to show that he was responding to these constituents' concerns. It was in moves like this that community groups traded in political capital and became part of a human infrastructure that maintained the city's official image of itself.

"Human infrastructure" is the term I use to describe how social networks make particular actions seem possible or impossible. The concept formed at the intersection of my activist engagements and scholarly research. Through my anthropology program at UC Irvine, I found some great work on creative urban survival by ethnographers AbdouMaliq Simone and Filip De Boeck. They both wrote about how in Kinshasa, Democratic Republic of Congo, they saw people take over the work of infrastructure. When physical systems fell apart or went offline, underlying social networks kept goods and services flowing. This reminded me of the survival cycling I saw in L.A. I also knew that riding bikes was easier if you knew other people who rode bikes. That was why I had moved to the Ecovillage, so I could live in a social environment where I wasn't a freak for riding a bike. Our relationships with friends and family form systems through which we share ideas and values. We help each other through this social scaffolding; we are disconnected from each other where it's lacking.

Human infrastructure shapes not only our ideas about mobility, but also the experiences we have in public spaces. Certainly there are material effects when millions of residents habitually fill streets with their cars. There's plenty of public and political recognition of car culture's effects on air pollution and traffic congestion, but not as much awareness about its destructive effects on place. Because riding a bicycle had put my focus on the power of an individual body and the social effects of our choices, I theorized that this was one level at which to combat car culture, simply choosing to travel differently. But because traveling differently was so stigmatized in L.A., new human infrastructure was needed to support it.

There were a few good reasons to pursue a human-infrastructure strategy in adapting to sustainable transportation. First of all, it was less resource-intensive. Unlike the fixed, large-scale systems that allow us to access resources in isolation from the ecological costs of their extraction, human infrastructure systems get remade and transformed every day simply through how we interact with each other.[34] Secondly, we had a good start with the L.A. bike movement. All the activists I knew who were dedicated to shifting transportation norms in Los Angeles formed a human infrastructure that made it possible for us to value bicycling in this place hostile to it. We looked to each other for validation. We confirmed to each other that the judgment and the exposure were worth the feeling we got from riding our bikes. We made it normal to ride bicycles in Los Angeles. We weren't waiting for the city to redesign the streets before we ditched our cars, even though our efforts suggested that we thought everyone else was.

Human infrastructure shapes policy decision making, but is itself rarely seen as meriting public investment, which tends to go into brick-and-mortar projects. It can be invisible to the people using and creating it because it just feels natural. Because of their combined focus on activist strategy and street life, my two fieldwork projects slowly revealed to me how people act as infrastructure, both physically in terms of how we traveled and politically as networks through which information and power flowed. City of Lights carried the embodied knowledge of jornalero cyclists into local bike advocacy through LACBC staff like Allison and Dorothy, and volunteers like me. CicLAvia represented a temporary interruption of the usual human infrastructure of the streets, taking motorized travel out of the equation. The event was supposed to make these relations visible, and then maybe the

---

34 My understanding of the role of everyday life in shaping our world came through the work of the French theorist Pierre Bourdieu, who I'd been reading since my undergraduate days. Bourdieu had some great insights into the reproduction of culture, especially in his work on practice (lived routines) and performances of good taste. In Bourdieu's writing I found explanations both for how travel behavior emerged from transportation culture and how social capital flowed through human networks.

activists, the electeds, and the public would agree that investing in human infrastructure was vital to sustainable transportation.

Forget funding bike lanes, what we needed were bike crews at every high school; co-ops at every community center; stipends for the old guys who repaired bikes for kids in their neighborhoods. We needed to pay poor people for using bicycles and being a part of the growing network through which more sustainable transportation cultures could flow. What more direct action could there be to disrupt the usual devaluation of people who used bikes to survive?

This alternative to the bike infrastructure strategy was coalescing through my studies and activism, but it really came together in the summer of 2010, when I got a grant to investigate human infrastructure for bicycling in a few cities to compare with what I'd seen in Los Angeles.[35] Traveling was a relief because my relationship had ended and as many hopes as I had for CicLAvia, I felt dislocated at home. I returned to Detroit, where I had done some fieldwork in 2009, and it was in Detroit's empty streets that I noticed how unnecessary traffic infrastructure is when there are no crowds to organize. And without traffic pressure, I noticed my body's power more, since riding a borrowed bike always brings my attention to the bodily experience of bicycling. There are riding skills I've developed intuitively over years of riding, such as how to lean into turns and when to shift gears. On an unfamiliar machine I have to exercise these skills differently.

Having had the chance to ride without traffic in Detroit, I felt more clearly that the thing I wanted to change was transportation culture, and that street design alone was not the tool for the job. When I'm waiting at a red light on my bike it's not the markings on the street that make me feel out of place. I feel out of place because the driver behind me is honking. He's honking because

35 I received a New Approaches to Individualization, Infrastructure, and Consumption Fellowship supported by Intel Labs and the Institute for Money, Technology and Financial Inclusion at UC Irvine.

I'm blocking his path. Doesn't changing street design so that we won't interact at all sidestep the roots of this hostility? What we needed to undo, I felt, was the decision to let the blasé attitude drive us far, far apart.

But even in Detroit, the infrastructure strategy was visible. There was a brand new, empty bike/ped bridge and a rail-to-trail conversion, the Dequindre Cut, that had gotten a lot of attention. It struck me as odd to spend money on separated infrastructure when there weren't floods of people to separate. The purpose of street redesign as I understood it was to make bicyclists safer so that more people had more transportation options. What were these empty infrastructures in Detroit supposed to achieve? The strategy of "if you build it, they will come" meant something different here; it wasn't about drawing people out of their cars, it was a strategy for drawing newcomers to a particular place. Maybe these big projects weren't for Detroit's current residents at all.

One day I rode my borrowed bike from where I was staying in Corktown to the Henry Ford Museum in Dearborn. I passed through an industrial landscape backed by a skyline of slim towers, and since there was plenty of room for the semi trucks to pass me, it wasn't an unpleasant trip. When I reached my destination, I was surprised to find Greenfield Village, Henry Ford's nostalgic vision for small-town America. I'd never heard of it. Inside, there was a penny-farthing bicycle and a man paid to ride it, blacksmithing demonstrations, and little cottages to walk through. I had not expected to stumble onto a theme park where the titan of industry who had most successfully propagated mass production memorialized the slower pace of small-town life. I mean, it was precisely the popularity of Ford's industrial products that narrowed our cultural ideas about what social life could happen in a street. What was this place?

Greenfield Village sat behind walls that hid the vast industrial zone surrounding it, and as I walked through its hodgepodge of preserved Americana, I thought about the disconnect between consumerism and its drain on the world's collective resources. The look, the feel, matter more than the underlying and often ugly social relations. Growing up in the United States, we learn that life is best lived on a cloud of comfort where only imagination, not energy, limits our pleasure/freedom. And it's not just us. Globally, success means getting on the consumer side so you can leave the ugly side behind. The divide hurts so many people but very few turn around to dismantle it once they've crossed it; they're too busy trying to give their kids an easier time.

It's difficult to get out of that mentality because we're social creatures. If you try to consume less, people sometimes react to you like you're a privileged jerk. Five years into being a bike commuter, I knew that this act came across as smug. Once I mentioned riding a bike, or when they saw my bike or some related accessory, strangers thought it was okay to unload their contempt for bicycling onto me in polite conversation. This happened even more once I got a sharrow tattoo on my left calf in July 2010.[36] The bike thing evoked a defensive reaction, as though I'd announced my moral superiority (I think vegetarians and vegans probably know what I'm talking about here). Since I'm an ethnographer who is curious about people's transportation preferences, I didn't see these unsolicited opinions as a personal attack so much as research.

I have had many people, totally unprompted, tell me why they don't bike. They tell me how they wish they could, because they feel guilty about their carbon footprint, but it's too dangerous. (Then later maybe they'll recount, offhand, the gruesome details of the most recent car crash that traumatized them.) I've noticed that this defensive response happens more often with women, I

36 A sharrow is a road marking painted on travel lanes that shows an outline of a bicycle with two chevrons above it.

think because we are socialized to expect judgment from those around us so we feel we have to justify why we are living the way we do.

When I started bike commuting in 2005, it felt like for the first time I could put my foot down and touch the ground. Traveling that way gave me a basis for developing an awareness of what resources I was using on a daily basis. I wanted to share this with my fellow Angelenos through CicLAvia, which was designed to plant the seed for better L.A. street life norms on an individual and social level. At the individual level, the event could be a vehicle for getting in touch with a sense of bodily power. At the social level, it asserted that in this space it was actually more appropriate to be outside of a car. Open street events offered the opportunity to experience life beyond Autopia without having to reject car culture as people try out an embodied relationship with bicycling in a semi-controlled environment. Maybe attendees wouldn't even notice how transgressive they were being, since biking in a crowd is fun. They could start shedding the protective layers of consumer waste without missing them. By creating a more welcoming space in which individuals could experience bicycling instead of relating to it as a disconnected image, maybe CicLAvia could shift the culture so that bicycle users didn't have to face being treated like dirt anymore.

The first CicLAvia closed seven and a half miles of streets in Los Angeles from 11 am until 3 pm on Sunday, October 10, 2010 (10-10-10). An estimated 30,000 to 40,000 people rode bikes or walked along the route, which passed from historically Chicano Boyle Heights in East L.A., through Little Tokyo and Downtown L.A., into Central American MacArthur Park and Koreatown, and ending at East Hollywood's Bicycle District, a hub for the cycling community in central Los Angeles. Jaime had come up from Bogotá for the event, and was one of the speakers at the press conference the mayor held at the Boyle Heights end of the route. It was nice to see his role as a visionary recognized.

There have been at least two CicLAvia events each year since its first iteration, and it has shifted routes to connect new parts of the city through close collaboration with community-based organizations. We'd grafted the bogotano event onto the Angeleno landscape and the hybridization took, to the surprise of many. At each CicLAvia I've attended, I've enjoyed the crowded bottlenecks where so many people have shown up that we have to walk our bikes, and the long stretches in between where I can ride fast and the street is quiet. Since I was only one of the people who created CicLAvia, and since I haven't been part of its production since 2011, I can't say that I fully recognize my vision in what the event became. But I hope that for some it can be a place to analyze the intersection of race and transportation in Southern California.

Feeling small in the face of overconsumption and its effects on our world, I found a sense of strength in the do-it-yourself practice of being a bike commuter. I could see that feeling strong on a bike was far outside the norm for people of color in my home region, due to a number of factors. So I'd developed a dissertation project that centered on changing the low status of bicycling in Los Angeles. After three years, fate pulled me away, and I wrapped up my fieldwork and left L.A. within a few months of the first CicLAvia. While other co-founders moved on to closer relationships with local government agencies and developed CicLAvia into the semi-regular event it is today, I cloistered myself and spent several years analyzing L.A.'s bike world a thousand miles away in Seattle. I built a new network of activist and researcher peers, and they helped me understand that most bicycle advocates weren't strategizing for a multiracial public the way I was. This pushed my work in a new direction as I focused more on undoing racial segregation's effects on the bike movement than on undoing car culture at large. By the time I'd finished writing up my dissertation, I knew that what we needed was a multiracial movement; what I didn't know was how much resistance I would find in my fellow bike advocates.

Part Two

Building a Multiracial Movement

Writing

Up

8

When I left L.A. for Seattle in 2011, I thought it would be a good idea to step away from the action and move into a sylvan writer's retreat. I needed to get away from the hubbub of my bike life in order compose a dissertation about it, and Seattle held the person I was more drawn to than anyone else. But up north, I quickly got depressed. In the dissertation process, "writing up" is a good time to be surrounded by peers, cohort-mates who understand the craft of separating out the threads of your impressions of the world ("fieldwork data") and weaving them together with the fibers harvested from your endless review of how others have analyzed cultural life ("the literature"). However, in leaving L.A., I had removed myself from my Southern California university circle. Then a month after I moved to Seattle in what turned out be an unusually long, rainy winter, the earthquake in Japan and subsequent nuclear disaster at Fukushima terrified me. For weeks I lived with more anxiety than I'd ever experienced. I was in an environment so much cleaner and greener than where I'd lived in L.A., and yet I felt like our world was on the brink of absolute crisis.

I found a therapist to wrestle with my anxiety, but I knew I needed more to feel anchored in this unfamiliar city. At first I thought since I wouldn't be doing fieldwork in Seattle, I had no need to seek out a bike scene. But I never found the key to my bike lock after I moved, and finally went to Bike Works in Columbia City to get a new one. In their scruffy shop in an old yellow house, I felt at home in a way that I hadn't since leaving the Ecovillage. I'd also been observing street life and wanted to compare notes with people who knew biking in this hilly city better than me. I reached out to Tom Fucoloro of *Seattle Bike Blog* and we met for coffee in the U-District one afternoon. He knew of CicLAvia and wanted to hear all about it, which meant a lot to lonely me.

I also sent some emails to people at Bike Works, and got a response from someone with the unlikely name of Davey Oil. I made an appointment to meet and liked Davey immediately. We jumped into a long conversation about our ideals for bike activism (Bike education as a means to fight oppression: yes!; Biking as an exclusive subculture: no!), and he explained the work he'd been doing as the volunteer coordinator at Bike Works for several years. A skilled mechanic, Davey hosted a weekly event at Bike Works called the Volunteer Repair Party (VRP). Unlike the bike co-ops in L.A., Bike Works was not a place where you brought in your own bike to repair. They used the "recycle-a-bicycle" model, where donated bikes are refurbished and sold or taken home by the kids who learned to repair them. These youth-centered earn-a-bike programs were happening all over the country, it turned out. Bike Works also hosted an annual bike swap where kids could bring in a bike they'd outgrown and take home a bigger one. Some of the preliminary repair work happened at the VRPs. Regardless of what I knew about wrenching, Davey assured me, I was welcome to show up and knowledgeable people would help me as needed to get the little bikes in working order.

Once I started volunteering, I could see that Davey didn't just keep track of volunteer hours and positions; he kept people excited and involved. He made every volunteer feel like the few hours s/he gave to the organization were a vital contribution. I noticed early on that I was not the only person energized by Davey's personality. Every time I went to a Bike Works event, I watched how people's faces lit up when they talked to him. Davey invited Tom and me to Critical Mass one month, and the three of us ended up at Gas Works Park, watching the glowing Seattle skyline. Then we biked back up to Capitol Hill through Interlaken Park, lights off for the maximum effect of the damp green darkness of the urban forest. By the time the three of us organized a ride in September 2011 to mourn recent bicyclists' deaths, I felt less like an impotent bystander to cascading ecological disaster and more like I was part of an activist network. These relationships trickled like a creek into my dissertation desert and helped me hone the concept of human infrastructure that had become central to my project.

Bike networks helped me to find research peers, too. Through the British email list Cycling and Society, I met a few other graduate students who, like me, were studying the cultural and social aspects of bicycling rather than street design or engineering (the usual fields for bicycle researchers). Two of them were Sarah McCullough, who was writing a dissertation about the origins of mountain biking in Marin County, California, and Lusi Morhayim, who was writing about bicycling and public space in San Francisco. The three of us started an email list called Bicicultures at the end of 2011. We pooled our contacts and quickly built up to over 100 subscribers. Many Biciculturistas were also activists engaged locally with a social justice-oriented bike project like a repair cooperative or a youth program. It made my dissertation writing less isolating to be part of an interdisciplinary conversation about what bicycling meant in different times and places.

Meeting weekly with Tom and Davey to discuss bikes and culture change also helped me get some perspective on what had been unique about the bike work I had done in Los Angeles. I collaborated with plenty of people of color as a bike activist and researcher in L.A. without thinking there was anything exceptional about that. In Seattle, there were lots of white people enthusiastic about bicycling and marshaling public resources toward it, but that didn't mean they saw it as a racial or environmental justice issue. By May 2012, I was reflecting on my blog that "the bike movement has not done enough to confront and question the ways that transportation fits into long histories of discrimination and injustice in America."

As I developed this understanding of the bike movement, I was disappointed to learn that my collaborators back in L.A. were getting pushed out of bicycle advocacy. City of Lights had expanded from giving out lights to partnering with a community-based organization, the Instituto de Educacion Popular del Sur de California (IDEPSCA), to create a tool library and workshop space at their worker center in downtown L.A. Because of its core focus on individuals already using bikes as a survival strategy, City of Lights was building relationships with networks beyond what bicycle advocates had considered relevant to their cause. Despite this coalition work, the City of Lights campaign ended at the Los Angeles County Bicycle Coalition in the first half of 2012 when the organization pushed out Andy Rodriguez, who had stepped into Allison Mannos' role managing the campaign when she moved on. A Latino City of Lights organizer who was on the LACBC board of directors told me that he felt pressured to resign. The organization wanted to keep the City of Lights name and all grant funding the project team had secured. The explanation I heard from friends was that the organization saw the project's focus on racial inclusion as too far afield, as though City of Lights was going in some new direction that didn't fit at LACBC.

This made no sense to me because we'd always been openly focused on racial inclusion. Had the organization's leadership been in denial about this for nearly four years? The executive director had supported us through a tough moment at the end of 2009 when staff with the national grant program Advocacy Advance told us that we were misguided in focusing on communities of color. LACBC's website prominently featured Allison's work on a coalition campaign to get a bike lane on Seventh Street. And yet our guiding values were now presented as new and unwelcome. All I could figure was that City of Lights had never been incorporated into the organization's mission, and eventually this benign neglect, compounded with cultural differences among the individuals involved, sowed miscommunication. The former City of Lights crew bonded over their dispossession and went on to become a new entity, Multicultural Communities for Mobility (MCM), signaling that they planned to tackle more street and transportation issues beyond bicycling.

While my L.A. collaborators organized to keep their work going on their own terms, I wondered whether we were the only bike activists who wanted to build coalitions with justice-centered movements. One way to explore this question was to learn what community activists in social justice movements in my current city thought about bicycling, and bring their insights to the attention of bike advocates. In the spring of 2012, I secured funding from Bike Works and an organization then called the Bicycle Alliance of Washington to conduct interviews that would lead to some outreach recommendations. I wanted to show that people form opinions about bicycling in the context of their own lives and landscapes, and if bicycle advocates wanted to appeal to more city dwellers, surely we could benefit from gathering perspectives on bicycling from those who worked in community justice spaces.

I found interviewees through volunteer work with community-based organizations in Rainier Valley, where Seattle's most ethnically diverse neighborhoods could be found and which was an active site of tensions around gentrification. By August 2012, I had completed nine interviews for what I called the Seattle Bike

Justice Project. I got to hear stories about biking in Compton and Addis Ababa. A few people said they'd like to bike, while others felt resentful of white bicyclists' entitled attitudes. I decided to make the information I had gathered available as a public resource.[37]

The interview project moved my activism further away from bicycle promotion and more toward the need for cross-cultural understanding within the bike movement itself. Even though there were networks of people who shared views about what actions would improve and expand bicycling, we didn't all see it the same way. For me, bicycling symbolized liberation from destructive systems. For others, it might be a temporary source of savings that actually helped them become consumers in those destructive systems, an uncomfortable speed bump on the road to the good life. For still others, it's just a fun way of getting around, as disconnected from economic hardship as they are. I started out wanting to change how people interacted in streets, but now I wanted to change how my fellow activists developed a shared agenda that included or excluded different kinds of travelers.

Sarah McCullough and I decided to organize a multi-city bike research conference we called the Bicicultures Roadshow for March 2013. We were both close to finishing our dissertations, and we wanted to stage some events that illuminated how ethnographic fieldwork can link together activist and academic networks. With English bike geographer Peter Wood, we spent some time in L.A. and Davis, riding bikes and talking about them with scholars and advocates. In L.A., we held a bike movement oral history night at the L.A. Ecovillage that LACBC co-founder Ron Milam facilitated. Following the L.A. bike movement narrative my own fieldwork had traced, from Critical Mass to the Bike Kitchen

37 The website for the Seattle Bike Justice Project (seattlebikejustice.wordpress.com) has demographic information about who I interviewed, what their responses were, and suggestions about how bicycling can help build community. I highly recommend taking on a project like this for anyone who wants to learn about the diversity of views on bicycling in a given place, but before you do, get some training in listening without disagreeing.

to Midnight Ridazz to CicLAvia, we invited a few speakers to talk about the early days of these projects. It was a public event where anybody could contribute to a timeline we pasted up on the walls around the lobby.

It turned out that in tracing the contours of the movement I'd been part of in L.A., I was also seen as reinforcing its boundaries. Sarah and I had designed an open and collaborative space, but I heard through the grapevine that some people felt excluded by the fact that there were invited speakers. A few people who showed up seemed like they didn't expect to be welcome there, which I think was a product of how combative L.A.'s bike movement can feel. For my part, I was willing to acknowledge that I knew only one sliver of L.A.'s bike scenes. Activism can be hyper-local, and within the enormous city of course there were other bike networks beyond what I knew. From then on I was careful to talk about my research as centered in my perspective, not attempting a comprehensive history of some official L.A. bike movement.

I made the timeline into an online resource and invited anyone to submit items. I never got many submissions, though, which to me emphasized the importance of offline relationships in uncovering marginal experiences. The whole thing also revealed to me that bigger frameworks of social power and privilege penetrate even into activist spaces where people feel like the underdog. At our Bicultures symposium in Davis, I cringed when a white woman panelist, who was a feminist icon in the bike movement, pointed her finger at a black woman in the audience and demanded to hear her thoughts on race. My fellow bike activists might see themselves as the little guy, without the self-awareness to notice their other forms of privilege. Feeling like you belonged in the bike movement seemed to stem more from the shared experience of white middle-class security than from using a bicycle; I could now see this after my weeks on the road with Bicultures.

I'd been talking to bike activists, I'd been talking to researchers, and I'd been talking to community activists outside of the bike movement. The final section of the human infrastructure that has given me a voice within organized bicycling dropped into place when I was invited to meet a multiracial network of bike advocates who had been strategizing together for years. In early 2013, I got an email from someone named Hamzat Sani who was assembling an "equity advisory council" (EAC) for the League of American Bicyclists (LAB) in Washington, D.C. Did I want to be part of the group? I said yes, wondering what would unfold. I had heard about LAB peripherally over the years, mainly because of their bike safety education classes and because of their system for rating how "bike friendly" cities were. I knew people who had attended their National Bike Summit, which included bike advocacy and planning workshops and a day of lobbying members of Congress.

LAB, the oldest bicycle advocacy organization in the country, flew EAC members to D.C. to participate in a retreat and the National Bike Summit. Our meeting took place in a windowless room at the conference hotel. I remember walking into a room where I didn't know anybody, seeing their camaraderie, and feeling shy. But they welcomed me into their ranks. Of the people there who continued as the EAC, there were Anthony Taylor from the Twin Cities, Elizabeth Williams from Long Beach, Neil Walker from Atlanta, Brian Drayton from the Bay Area, Eboni Senai Hawkins from Chicago, Helen Ho and Devlynn Chen from New York City, and Keith Holt from Milwaukee. The facilitators were Hamzat, LAB communications director Carolyn Szczepanski, and LAB board member Alison Hill Graves. Carolyn and Alison were the only white people in the room.

The two of them had been in dialogue about starting a program focused on diversity at LAB in 2012 when Hamzat showed up with some specific ideas. He had recently returned home to D.C. from Atlanta, where he had co-founded a local chapter of the black-community bike ride Red, Bike and Green.[38] The EAC had been organized primarily by Hamzat and Carolyn, and they'd invited many of the members of a collective called United Cycling Voices. Some EAC members were also part of the National Brotherhood of Cyclists, which was a network of black and multiracial bike clubs that honored the legacy of black cycling champion Marshall "Major" Taylor.[39] I hadn't even imagined that there were organized efforts to diversify bicycle advocacy already going on, so I felt pretty glad I'd started to think out loud about these issues on my blog and that a few key people were reading.

The EAC theory was that in changing an established bike advocacy institution we could, by extension, transform its broader network of clubs and organizations as well. To this end, the EAC was invited to review LAB's programming and recommend changes that would make the organization more inclusive. The day passed quickly as Hamzat, Carolyn, and Alison provided background on these programs and we discussed what equity, diversity, and inclusion should mean for a national bicycle advocacy organization. Once the bike summit began the next day, I felt a little daunted. As I knew from fieldwork around the country, people of color riding bicycles was hardly unusual; in fact, there might even be more of us than white people using bicycles as a transportation solution. However, people of color speaking for bicycling was not the norm. The conference and lobby day at Congress were very white. There were just a few other people of color in attendance beyond the

38 RBG emerged in Oakland in 2007, the brainchild of Jenna Burton. Their rides focused on celebrating and exploring black neighborhoods and senses of place. I started hearing about it once I lived in Seattle, which is also when I learned about the East L.A. Chicana collective Ovarian Psycos. Eboni, who I met on the EAC, had taken RBG to Chicago with her when she moved there from Oakland, and as others developed local rides they coordinated through a national network of mostly women organizers.

39 To learn more about Major Taylor's legacy see Andrew Ritchie's biography *Major Taylor: The Fastest Bicycle Rider in the World* and the website for the Major Taylor Association based in Massachusetts.

EAC members, like Yolanda Davis-Overstreet, a filmmaker and central figure in both United Cycling Voices and the National Brotherhood of Cyclists.

As discouraging as it felt to witness the gap between who rides and who speaks for riding, at least others already saw this as a problem. The racial homogeneity of the National Bike Summit had even spurred the creation of a whole new conference called the Youth Bike Summit, after two students who felt out of place at the D.C. event planned a different kind of gathering on their way home to New York.[40] YBS started in 2011 and brought together earn-a-bike youth participants and program staff from around the country. Maybe the EAC could help make LAB into a similarly multiracial space.

Once I knew that there was a conversation for me to join, I got bolder in using my blog to try and show where race, inequality, and bicycling intersected. I felt a little uneasy about it, though. *Urban Adonia* had previously showcased the logistics of how I made it work to live carfree in Los Angeles. I wasn't afraid to bash car culture online, but I was very anxious about bringing up racism to an audience of my fellow bike advocates. Even as I got positive feedback for voicing dynamics that others had also noticed, I still felt worried every time I clicked the publish button. I didn't want to lose my place in this movement that mattered so much to me; at the same time I didn't quite trust that it had my back.

---

40 There's an essay by Pasqulina Azzarello, Jane Pirone, and Allison Mattheis about the creation and philosophy of the Youth Bike Summit in the 2016 book I co-edited, *Bicycle Justice and Urban Transformation*.

Bicycle
Gentrification

9

The most glaring evidence that bicycle advocacy was out of sync with justice-centered movements lay in the rapidly growing association between gentrification and bike infrastructure. Back in early 2008, I'd witnessed homeowners in Long Beach complaining that a bike boulevard would lower their property values, because they saw cycling for transportation as a low-class practice. By March 2010, I was hearing the opposite from a leading figure in urban design.

I had biked across central L.A. with a group of friends to attend the keynote address of the L.A. StreetSummit, a conference of activists and professionals organized by Occidental College's Urban and Environmental Policy Institute. Occidental sits on one of the hills that make up the Eagle Rock neighborhood in northeast L.A. (north of downtown, east of the L.A. River). Starting from my home a few miles southwest, we climbed over the hills of Silver Lake, passing iconic mid-century homes worth millions, skirting the reservoir path where fit people jog with their dogs. Dropping down to cross the river and the Interstate 5 freeway, we passed businesses with Spanish names that catered to a Latino clientele. Our group met up with more people at Flying Pigeon, a bike shop in the Highland Park neighborhood that had been started by a founder of the bike repair collective next door, the Bike Oven. We climbed the final hill at dusk, circling through a neighborhood of

1920s bungalows where the roar of the highway dominated the dry air.

The speaker that night was Janette Sadik-Khan. As Transportation Commissioner of New York City, she had shut down Times Square to automotive traffic, spreading beach chairs so that pedestrians could enjoy the space. Sadik-Khan, with the encouragement of a sympathetic mayor, set about making New York a bike friendly city, and became a celebrity in the sustainable transportation movement. Her actions as commissioner demonstrated what many urban planners and activists believe: streets made welcoming to all modes of transport make better public spaces. She showed us slides demonstrating the efficiency of using bikes and feet to get around crowded cities.

During the Q&A, Sadik-Khan took a question from the balcony above the main hall, and I looked up to see the speaker. He was a young black man who spoke nervously, as people often do in front of large crowds, about the changes in his neighborhood that seemed to come along with new bike lanes. He made a connection between bicycle infrastructure on public streets, our supposed goal as advocates for urban transport cycling, and gentrification. Sadik-Khan barely missed a beat and launched into a comparison of the high costs of transportation with high housing costs. Lowering transportation costs by making it possible for people to get around on bikes would make their incomes more available for housing costs. Then she moved on to other questions, seemingly satisfied that she had dismissed his concerns about gentrification.

As I sat there trying to parse what had made my heart beat faster, I heard Sadik-Khan mention a curious fact. After her department made improvements to Bryant Park in Manhattan, property values in the area went up 225%. Clearly the message seemed to be that there was no contradiction between investing in public space and a robust real estate market. I understood the young man who'd asked the question to be framing bike infrastructure as another iteration of the reality that city changes aren't meant to benefit people like him. Bike infrastructure was being used as a form of urban renewal. That man's question helped me see something troubling in the movement I'd been thinking of as my own for several years.

I believed that in order to raise the status of bicycling, we needed to build coalitions with other movements committed to a more just world. We needed to demonstrate how bicycling could be a tool for community resilience. What I heard at Sadik-Khan's talk was that another way to raise bicycling's value was to encourage its association with trendy urban design. Once I heard her make that connection, I saw how widespread this project already was. Recreational cycling was a rich man's pastime; all advocates had to do was extend its elite image to bicycle transportation. They could do this by telling mayors that bike infrastructure would improve neighborhoods. They could show the creative class on bicycles, riding happily to their tech and graphic design jobs. Had the bike movement jumped on the development bandwagon with no analysis of how its strategies played out in landscapes of inequality?

I originally thought that bicycle gentrification was a side effect of an ill-considered strategy. I had taken it for granted from the beginning of my project that since bicycling was often a response to economic necessity, we needed to be careful to avoid bike projects that would negatively impact low-income people. Humans have an ingenious ability to subvert the intended use of objects and designed spaces, and for me, bicycling was a way to witness and disrupt inequality. But a number of other researchers I spoke with, including PhD students and Biciculturistas Melody Hoffmann in Minneapolis and John Stehlin in Berkeley, confirmed that, yes, advocates were promoting bicycle gentrification. And, yes, associating bicycling with whiteness and economic security also meant associating the spaces designed for it with a new colonial urbanism. In an era of rising housing costs, gentrification, and displacement, the bike movement chose an advocacy strategy blatantly promoting neighborhood change.[41]

Because I'd been learning about the colonial control embedded in urban planning and design since my undergraduate studies, I did not see "good design" as an end in itself, or as something that could fix social problems on its own.[42] I knew that many advocates were committed to transforming public spaces and they wanted this transformation to happen in accordance with spatial controls they had seen in Northern European cities. To my ear, this now sounded like a new refrain of the old colonial strategy of managing populations through structuring their living spaces. These communities could not be trusted to manage themselves, so resources had to be doled out on their behalf as the conquerors saw fit. Green infrastructure like cycle tracks extended this division and called it a social good. Investing buildings and engineered environments with the power to control human behavior, what the urban theorist David Harvey has called "environmental determinism," leaves the spark of life out of the picture. Focusing on urban design, rather than the people who inhabit and produce places, all too easily naturalizes their market-driven displacement.

I also wondered why bike advocates thought the physical infrastructure needed to come first. I'd found historical evidence

41 Melody Hoffmann and I co-authored an academic article where we traced examples of influential people praising bicycle infrastructure projects for contributing to rising property values. Our article, "Who is 'World Class'? Transportation Justice and Bicycle Policy," was published in the journal *Urbanities* in 2014. Melody's dissertation analyzed bicycle gentrification in the Twin Cities and Portland and her book on the subject, *Bike Lanes Are White Lanes*, came out in 2016.

42 For an example of an urban anthropologist analyzing the colonial project embedded in development and planning, see Farha Ghannam's 2002 book *Remaking the Modern*.

that shifts in popular attitudes toward transportation could result in changes to street design, not just follow from them. The birth of car culture illustrated that a mode of transportation could go viral before infrastructure had been built to accommodate it en masse. In Los Angeles, public support for driving predated public investment in car-specific street and highway design.[43] The first real pressure to spend public money on widening roads for a growing number of private automobiles began in the 1920s when a traffic crisis developed. Newspapers and auto clubs agreed that L.A. could not become one of the world's leading cities without adopting car-centric urban design because a modern city was one accessed by car. They urged the city to create a transportation plan that would accommodate driving above all else. This was seen as an evolution, and getting away from the city was seen as a good choice. Greater freedom of mobility would be a boon. The drivers had come; it was time to build for them.

Today, nostalgia around L.A.'s streetcars tends to obscure what really happened. Enthusiasts like to blame the end of streetcars on an auto industry conspiracy to destroy public transit. *Who Framed Roger Rabbit?*, a Disney movie from 1988, provides many people with their view of streetcar history. In that film, a cruel capitalist profits off the destruction of a beloved trolley system. In real life, during the 1920s traffic crisis, L.A. voters saw the private street railways as greedy corporate interests and decided against the city purchasing the networks. It's true that General Motors later came in and purchased the failing streetcar lines, dismantled them, and replaced them with National Trust Line buses, as they did in many cities. It's true that powerful media interests lobbied in favor of drivers. But the demand for private mobility environments wasn't car industry propaganda; our own families were the flesh and blood villains. I don't see car dependence as

---

43 Again following Scott Bottles' research here ; see Footnote 17.

a crime committed by corporate interests; rather, the American public chose it enthusiastically. Our choices created large-scale ecological problems, and we also chose suburban sprawl that was racially segregated by design.

The bike world seemed to prefer the Roger Rabbit version of what went wrong with our development pattern. True urban Progress could still be achieved if we undid the nefarious work of the auto industry and liberated streets through human-scale design. *If you build it, they will come* called the humans forth from their suburbs because the empty city was finally worth living in again. From this standpoint, the trolleys of Toon Town get to be the face of injustice, because urban renewal policies and the racist attitudes that buoyed them did such a thorough job of erasing the people who lived in cities. The bodies burdened by urban renewal were somehow less worth remembering than the old streetcars and buildings they'd inhabited.

Stories like those of Chávez Ravine's displaced families made me wary of efforts promoting design and the rhetoric of choice as pathways to sustainable transportation. The fixation with places over people manifests suburban segregation's effects on our society, where the urban underclass of immigrants and the native-born mired in generations of poverty inhabit city spaces without the political or social capital to influence decision making about how public resources get invested. The people with that influence have been isolated from forming strong social bonds with the people who live in the very spaces they want to transform.

By 2013, it looked to me like advocates either wanted to distance bicycling from marginal people who used it as a survival tool, or just didn't care how these survival cyclists fared. In any case, they were promoting gentrification as a good thing. Advocates seemed to want the public to view bicycling the way they did: as something for *normal* (i.e., white or at least economically secure) people, not something for the poor (who were probably black or brown). Increasing racial inclusion in the bike movement seemed like a way out of this corner where a homogenous group of strategists were blocking bicycling's potential as a transformative tool.

My dissertation, "Body-City-Machines: Human Infrastructure for Bicycling in Los Angeles," was in revisions, and I started operationalizing the human infrastructure theory on the monthly EAC strategy calls. Across the United States, people were making bicycling into a tool for community empowerment and fitting it into other kinds of identity, but it was hard to find financial support for expanding these efforts given the bike advocacy focus on street infrastructure. How could we influence bicycle advocacy to lobby for funding cross-cultural work that built popular demand, with more community members getting compensated?

In June 2013 my partner and I moved back to Portland, the city I'd missed so much back in my first year of graduate school. I started meeting more bike people, adding to those I knew from visiting over the years. I went to bike events and met with staff at environmental justice organizations like Verde and OPAL. But something didn't feel right. Portland was changing much faster than I'd realized and I had a hard time connecting with my sense of place there, even though the city had been my home for six formative years.

When a Florida court set Trayvon Martin's killer free that summer, an odd juxtaposition confronted me with how little advocates in this bicycling capital were connecting the dots between built environment change and urban displacement, and how as a result, safety for "cyclists" didn't look like safety for everyone. I wrote a blog post to try and organize my thoughts. This is from July 15, 2013:

It's about four and a half miles from downtown Portland to Peninsula Park up north. I made the trip on Sunday after attending a "bikes and economics" panel at the Portland Art Museum, riding to North Portland for a justice rally and march in response to Saturday's acquittal of the vigilante who left his car to stalk an African-American teenager walking alone in Florida last February. He was found not guilty even though he shot and killed the unarmed kid. With this news on my mind I felt strange about going to the panel at all, but I'd spent thirteen bucks on my ticket and I wasn't getting them back. So I put on a dress and crossed the river. In the museum auditorium, a white crowd of about forty fanned across the many rows of seats. Onstage were an elected official, Congressman Earl Blumenauer, beloved by the bike movement for his openly bikey stance on Capitol Hill; a city planner, Roger Geller, the bicycle coordinator for the Portland Bureau of Transportation; Elly Blue, a writer and publisher about to release her second book, *Bikenomics*; and the panel's moderator, Professor Jennifer Dill, a prominent bike researcher at Portland State University and the director of the Oregon Transportation Research and Education Consortium. When I started reading about Richard Florida's creative class theory in 2008, I thought maybe it was a coincidence that the bike movement's emphasis on infrastructure matched Florida's core idea: if you build it, they will come. That is, if politicians want to attract desirable, talented residents/consumers to their regions in the post-industrial, idea/upscale consumption economy, they must invest in the urban design elements that are as honey to these worker bees. Naw, I thought, the bike has way too much democratic potential to be reduced to a marketing tool. But I keep hearing powerful people like Congressman Blumenauer characterizing bike projects as a strategy to "attract talent," bringing "the best and the brightest" to places like Portland. In March, I heard the mayor of Indianapolis make similar remarks at the League of American Bicyclists' National Bike Summit that was this year themed "bikes mean business." I'm hearing a lot of consensus that a good way to convert people to bikes is to convince them that bike projects will raise their property values. It seems like the bike movement, or at least its policy arm, has decided that their goal of getting more people on bikes is not in conflict with the goal of making urban neighborhoods more expensive, and I am baffled by how openly they make this claim. Aren't policymakers and lobbyists supposed to at least pretend that their pet projects have benefits for more than one group? And shouldn't livable neighborhoods be affordable? Because we're not all homeowners, and I don't see a lot of value in rents that skyrocket because more people are choosing to ride bikes. Maybe the city should be compensating us urban cyclists for our contribution to the marketable landscapes they crave. If influential people have decided who, exactly, they want to attract to cycling, maybe the question we should be asking is if you build it, who will be replaced? The drive to bring in desirables leaves aside the question of who gets categorized as undesirable. I wonder if an unspoken goal of bike advocates uncomfortable with race, class, and cultural difference is to create urban zones free of these problems by simply vanishing, through the unquestionably objective means of the market, people unlike themselves. After all, using urban planning to rid cities of undesirables is nothing new. I hope, though, that folks will reconsider whether it is too hard to convince existing city residents that riding a bike is a good thing. Is it better that they be replaced by outsiders who already have that extra spending power to buy more bakfiets for the bicycle boulevard? I had a lot to think about as I rode up to North Portland, passing through the neighborhood around Emanuel Hospital that had been razed as an urban renewal zone in the 1970s, biking up the controversial lane on N Williams Avenue. I thought about Geller's comment that what we need here in Portland to really get more investment in bike infrastructure is an urban renewal zone. I believe he was referring to some local funding terminology, but why is such a loaded phrase still in official use? One community's Voldemort is another's Harry Potter, and it matters who gets to decide what is failed urban policy and what needs another try. At Peninsula Park, a group of several hundred people stood around a gazebo while speakers lined up to share their anger and concerns through a megaphone. One woman said that she saw a ride of 11,000 cyclists passing a few blocks away, but there were only a few hundred people here at the rally. I had seen the ride, too, and didn't put two and two together until later that it was Cascade Bicycle Club's Seattle to Portland ride arriving in the city. I thought it was a little unfair for her to single out cyclists as a group absent from the rally, considering how many people had biked there like myself. When we went out to march, we walked along Albina, then Killingsworth, then turned onto Vancouver. The stream of cyclists I'd seen earlier, and that the speaker had mentioned at the rally, was still trickling down Vancouver, against the flow of the demonstration. I was talking to friends when we heard shouting and saw a marcher using his body to block the path of a cyclist traveling in the bike lane. "Peace!" someone called out, as others intervened to end the altercation. "Peace!" In that moment, the distance between bike economics and social justice shrank to the distance between one frustrated man and the mobile symbol of a system stacked against him. Even if the city, the bike movement, the people in power who make funding decisions about street infrastructure, don't want to talk about the uneven politics of who gets to decide what transportation counts and who should benefit from improvements to public streets, the demonstrator blocking the path of the cyclist with his body made clear how this symbol of outside wealth stimulating the local economy, this "attractor of talent," the envy of Rahm Emanuel and other mayors who "want what Portland has," was too much to handle on a day when the country was mourning yet again the unequal treatment African-Americans can expect from our public institutions. It all comes together in the street, whether you're guiding the political machine and reaping the benefits or struggling as some undesirable who will soon be replaced by someone worth more. Because we all know that some bodies matter more than others.

I didn't know how this post would be received and I felt nervous about publishing it. It got some circulation, reposted by a few bike media outlets. It was encouraging that someone I'd mentioned in the post, Elly Blue, thanked me for writing it. Elly had been a college classmate and we'd kept in touch as she developed her reputation as a bike journalist and then publisher. When I moved back to Portland, she invited me to be part of her network focused on the feminist possibilities and challenges of bicycling. (She's even my editor on this book.) It seemed like there was room in the bike movement for my critical eye, and that I could do something useful with what I knew from my years as a bike ethnographer and observer.

In returning to the Pacific Northwest and writing my dissertation there, I saw in stark relief what I'd seen surfacing only occasionally in Los Angeles' sea of multiracial and multicultural urban movements: Plenty of people advocate for sustainability systems like bike infrastructure without considering the racism and wealth inequality embedded in how we plan and use urban space. Before we could effect change in transportation culture at large, we needed to build human infrastructure across the divide that had made the bike movement into a white-centered space, and that reverse white flight had exposed. I was more and more sure that increasing the diversity within bicycle advocacy would lead to different interventions designed to address the root causes of street contempt, and the national bike advocacy network seemed like a place to circulate ideas that banked on bicycling's cultural rather than economic value.

Then came the news from Carolyn and Hamzat that LAB received a grant to create a full-time position to run their Equity Initiative. Hamzat asked me to apply, and I did since I wasn't finding a lot of opportunities to use my new PhD. in Portland. As much as the city was a hub for bicycle research, I was at a loss to communicate the value of my anthropological approach to academic fields focused on the infrastructure strategy. The position in D.C. seemed like it would offer a great chance to study the human infrastructure of federal policy and to raise awareness about the links between street design and wealth inequality. I got the job, so my partner and I drove our life across the country to Washington, D.C. I wanted to make bicycling into something more rather than fewer people could access, and the most direct way I could think of to resist bicycle gentrification was to join the national bike advocacy network myself. I'd also fix its race problem along the way. Piece of cake.

Designing Bike Equity in the Shadow of White Supremacy

10

Starting the job at LAB in November 2013, I was a bundle of nerves. I worried about stepping into an office setting, having been on a self-directed academic journey for six years and fully without schedule for three. I was worried because I was hired to lead change, and I knew from past experience that hiring someone new to change an existing organization creates resistance. And most of all, I was worried because I was a Chicana anthropologist focused on human infrastructure, not a white person with a planning degree ready to fight for bike lanes. I held my breath and closed my eyes and hoped that my bike tattoo would make my loyalties clear.

The theory of the Equity Initiative was simple: a demographic shift was coming, and bicycle advocacy should be ready if we wanted bicycling to be part of the plural future. Prior to my hiring, Carolyn and Hamzat had released a report called "The New Majority" that continues to be cited because of its persuasive evidence that people of color are turning to bikes in greater numbers than white people. With this report they built on the research of Jay Townley, a bike industry consultant who had been working for years to show through numbers that women and people of color should be seen as important customers. And the deliverables for the grant project were straightforward. The idea was to make changes internally, document the process, and share it along the way with bike advocates around the country. We'd build momentum for bike equity within our social movement and provide organizational guidance with reports.

I met with staff to learn about their programs, taking copious notes and having fun brainstorming about possible changes. I worked closely with Carolyn and Jakob Wolf-Barnett, the chief operating officer. LAB's president, an Englishman named Andy Clarke, had been a figure in bicycle advocacy for many years and I hoped I'd get to learn about the history of the field from him. He was pleasant in my interview and first weeks in the office, seemingly content to play a background role in the Equity Initiative. My supervisor would be Jakob, who paired an interest in business innovations with an earnest commitment to experimenting until we got the equity work right.

My colleagues had varying levels of interest in what I'd been hired to do. One thing I grasped early on was that most of the staff of fifteen or so had not come up through a local bike movement. There was something of a split in the office between those were focused on making the organization more efficient because we wanted to make bicycling better and those who didn't want to change much about how they'd been doing their jobs for years. There were some moments of tension as I got to know my coworkers' personalities and tried to figure out how to balance their expectations of me with the job I'd been hired to do, but overall everybody was friendly and many people ate lunch together in the conference room.

A central task on my to-do list was working with internal leadership and the EAC to define the organization's commitment to equity. "Equity" was a popular buzzword in D.C. at the time, and influential groups like PolicyLink were promoting it as "the superior growth model." Integrating more people's needs into an organization's work was supposed to make it stronger overall. LAB was already participating in the Transportation Equity Caucus, co-convened by PolicyLink and The Leadership Conference on Civil and Human Rights. The Equity Caucus' monthly meetings took place in The Leadership Conference's offices in a building across K Street from ours, and brought together dozens of transportation, housing, labor, and disability rights groups. 2013 ended on a promising note when I started the Bike Equity Network email list to connect people interested in equity, diversity, and inclusion around bicycle advocacy, planning, and policy. It seemed like there was good support for developing what bike equity would mean within LAB.

At the board level, it turned out there was not clarity on what I had been hired to do. That first hit me when, early in 2014, I was asked to give a presentation to the board about the Equity Initiative, and was told to be careful in how I framed the project. If I had to market the program to board members, this suggested that they actually weren't all in support of it. That seemed less than ideal, but maybe getting board members excited about this was part of my job. I didn't think much of it at the time.

The board of directors was somewhat in disarray because most board members had been replaced in the last few years. LAB had just come out of a long fight over bike advocacy's aims. By the time I started studying them in 2008, bike advocates were at the tail end of a years-long disagreement over something called "vehicular cycling." The central point of conflict was whether there should be an infrastructure system for bicycling or if it was sufficient to offer education on how to "drive" a bicycle and ride in traffic like motor vehicles.

These positions called for different actions. In infrastructure-oriented advocacy, individuals are supposed to get to know political figures and their staff and build their political will to order and pay for street redesign. This strategy focuses on influencing the existing transportation planning process by lobbying for particular engineering projects, usually based on design models developed in Northern Europe. It is heavily associated with Portland, which has made bike infrastructure into one of its hallmarks. Bicycle gentrification was the product of this kind of bike advocacy. Alternatively, the vehicularist model focuses on education and assumes that motorists will make room if bicycle users ride predictably. I never took it on as an object of study, but to me it looked like the model was putting forth that people riding bikes should assert their right to occupy public space. I knew from bike friends that vehicular cycling had been popular since its introduction by bike enthusiast John Forester in the 1970s, and that it did not challenge the bias toward car infrastructure that was the norm in traffic engineering.

In practice, pretty much all of the bike activists I knew rode as vehicular cyclists, simply because we liked the freedom to ride where we chose rather than sticking in some official but inadequate network. Still, I stayed away from this heated debate when I saw it pop up in L.A., Seattle, and even at a bike conference in London. Watching white people shake with rage at each other from their two sides, neither of which represented people like me, I never felt the urge to pick a side. LAB was in the thick of it because it certified individuals to be League Cycling Instructors, or LCIs, and these educators were often vehicular cycling champions. At the same time, LAB had been supporting the growth of the national network of organized bicycle advocacy organizations focused on infrastructure development. The group also worked closely with the bike industry arm that funded advocacy, which had renamed itself PeopleForBikes around the time I started working in D.C. Disgruntled former LCIs continued to leave angry comments on LAB's website, but the leadership had decided in favor of the infrastructure side. The board of directors now reflected this.

I hadn't expected the vehicular cycling debate to be at all relevant to my work because it had nothing to do with underlying racialized inequalities. In the infrastructure paradigm, the high social status of driving was seen as something bicycling could match with some good marketing and its own purpose-built system. In the more bootstraps vehicularist framework, anyone who didn't feel comfortable taking over road space just needed to toughen up, never mind social conditioning to stay out of the way or fear of attracting police attention. The debate did trip me up, though, because it had closed the ranks of bike advocacy against a diversity of ideas. At LAB, promoting anything that wasn't physical infrastructure seemed to bring up fears that vehicularists were lurking in the background, spoiling for another fight. Good thing my job included movement-building beyond the organization, I figured. More and more people were joining the Bike Equity Network in early 2014, and we'd been hosting webinars and getting the word out about the Equity Initiative on social media. I started speaking at conferences and was invited onto advisory committees.

Through this networking, I realized that even though I'd only been in my position for a short time, people expected me to have "best practices" on bike equity hammered out. I usually recommended that advocates determine what worked best in their community through relationship building and co-creating their strategies and policy agendas. Yet over and over, I was asked to explain how already-designed bike trends like cycle tracks and bike share programs could be made equitable. Bike advocates expected me to be an expert in what environmental justice scholar Julian Agyeman has called "retrofitting equity": bringing in a person of color just before a project launches to fix deep-seated, structural inequalities embedded within the project's design.[44] Bike people expected me to have policy solutions they could use because they were convinced that working through the political system was the most important thing they could do. I'd hoped they would be more open to other ways of promoting bicycling.

My work was more focused on building movement networks than on trying to get the ear of powerful people, but if policy was more about who you knew than what you knew, maybe I should shift gears. So I was excited when Andy told me I would be joining him and our policy director at a meeting with the Secretary of Transportation, Anthony Foxx. When we were finally sitting in a conference room at the Department of Transportation, my heart was racing. It was a let-down, though, because both my colleagues from LAB and the staffers seemed to be going through the motions.

I remembered the first time I went to City Hall in Los Angeles, which was with organizers from the Bus Riders Union one morning in spring 2008. We were there to listen to a city budget hearing and to submit public comments in favor of transit funding. Besides the organizers, I was one of just two BRU members who had been able to make this weekday hearing. We went through security and headed for a hall one organizer described as a cathedral. Council Chambers were church-sized indeed, with murals encircling the ceiling, marble columns, and statuary. The council members present for the committee hearing sat casually in large, heavy wooden booths, some more elevated than others. The audience sat in wooden pews. Our party was clad in jeans and BRU t-shirts. All around us were bored-looking politicians and their aides, loafing in suits and heavy makeup. They were very much at home in this formal setting that was designed to awe. It

---

44 With fellow scholar Stephen Zavestoski, Agyeman is the creator of the blog *Invisible Cyclist*. His post on "retrofitting equity" was published there in July 2014.

worked on me; I felt uncomfortable at the thought of speaking in this room and having to address these superior beings. I could imagine my voice shaking and I envisioned their inattention. I'd never experienced a display of government power so distinctly before. It didn't make me want to become influential in that space, and I was glad I had to leave early.

At the meeting with Secretary Foxx, I thought I would be glimpsing the other side, where the real work happens. But when I tried to analyze the DOT meeting with my boss, he said there wasn't anything to discover. What I took from that was that he wasn't interested in plugging me into the network of relationships through which ideas flow and that makes things move in D.C. He and our policy director had the connections to stage a meeting like that, but it was a hollow performance. Either the real work happened between the individual organization and agency staff as friends, or LAB had no influence. In any case, I was left to interpret the meeting on my own, and the message I took away was that they didn't expect me to be a thinking partner. How was I supposed to make influential, closed networks like this into a vehicle for transportation culture change?

When I asked Keith Benjamin, my counterpart at another organization, for advice on policy, he told me that I should work on making my own connections in the D.C. equity landscape, building up political capital, which he called "juice." I'd seen juice in action at Transportation Equity Caucus meetings, where as a D.C. newcomer I had no intel to share and mostly twiddled my thumbs. I started attending events related to racial and environmental justice, trying to find avenues for collaboration. But when I chatted with other kinds of advocates, what I heard was that they saw bicycling as something for white men, not a cause for people of color.

The image of the entitled white cyclist, the exact thing I had been hired to help change, made it difficult for mestiza me to find allies in other areas. It obscured the reality of bicycling as a survival strategy for the same communities of concern that were the focus of transportation and environmental justice. Given the reasons why I got involved in bike advocacy, I felt offended by the assertion that I was fighting for a white man's cause. It was like I was being consumed by the shadow of white supremacy instead of shining a light. Granted, it is a long shadow; the association of bicycling with white entitlement is an old and enduring one. The more I learned about the history of the organized political movement to secure public resources for bicycle users, the more I questioned whether or not it actually had room for people like me.

For the National Bike Summit in 2014, I worked with planner Naomi Doerner to put together a historical overview of race and inclusion in the U.S. bike movement, in part to show the elitism from which the bicycle advocacy movement emerged. Bike technology was revolutionary when nineteenth century inventors started creating machines that expanded personal mobility. Bikes allowed individuals to travel farther, which could be a source of empowerment (for example, much has been made of U.S. feminists' early embrace of bicycling). LAB's predecessor, the League of American Wheelmen, was created in 1880 to push for improved roads and a national network of highways so that bicycle enthusiasts could travel farther. But this new freedom of mobility took shape in a racist and classist landscape.

Because the bicycle started as an expensive novelty, other street users saw its riders as privileged road hogs. As Bruce Epperson noted in his book on the development of the bicycle industry, *Peddling Bicycles to America,* "urban clashes were more frequently real or perceived class conflicts. . . Cyclists expected to be deferred to by their social inferiors on the street as they were in everyday life, while teamsters saw cyclists as effete dandies trying to dance around the edges of a street fight they didn't understand and couldn't protect themselves from." Bicycle enthusiasts expected other street users to adapt to their own ability for speed. Today's car culture was very much foreshadowed by this bicycle entitlement.

Early bicycling expressed the stark inequality of the time, including its outright racism. The presence of black people circulating on bicycles was alternately comical and offensive to whites. Researching the era at the Library of Congress, I found that the printmakers Currier & Ives had produced a comic series called "Darktown Bicycling" in the late 1890s, which depicted "darkies" wearing fine clothes and riding bicycles. The joke was that these uppity people would have the audacity to think that bicycling, a pastime of white leisure, was for them. Most significantly for the future of bicycle advocacy, the League of American Wheelmen voted to bar black members in 1894. This would suggest that marshaling public resources to improve bicycling was not about roads as public goods, but rather grew from these early advocates' sense of entitlement as moneyed whites.

When bicycles started to become more affordable due to mass production, Southern shop owners saw sales decline. Epperson shared the findings of an investigation by a Chicago bicycle manufacturer to discover why sales were falling in the south in 1897: "'as soon as the Negro took to sporting a wheel, just that soon did the fad cease among the southern whites . . . In New Orleans, in Birmingham and Nashville the business began to drop off perceptibly.' Working-class white Southerners were so bigoted that they wouldn't even ride in the same roadways as their black counterparts." Mass production made bicycles accessible to more people, which lowered the class associated with riding them and further exposed the racism of the time.

Despite early bicycle enthusiasts' views on who should and shouldn't ride, the bicycle became a popular transportation solution. With so many millions of machines available secondhand, people around the world have incorporated bicycles into all kinds of cultural settings. I think the racism in early bicycling has gone overlooked because the private car rapidly supplanted the bicycle as a mobile privilege machine and has held that place for a century. The bicycle became a hand-me-down technology suitable for the poor and the juvenile. Anyone who could afford to drive joined the white transportation class; those who could not traveled as best they could, often on two wheels. Accessing bicycling did not become a site of transportation justice the way that accessing public transit has been since the Montgomery bus boycotts, perhaps because the simple technology the underclass and immigrant poor inherited did not depend on sharing indoor space the way riding a bus or train did. Those bigoted, working-class, white southerners Epperson mentioned didn't have to keep riding alongside black counterparts once they could get inside the private space of a car. On car-dominated streets, being on a bike itself signified inferiority like being confined to the back of the bus did. Who would fight to keep people there?

Indeed, this was the message I was hearing from the transportation justice field: the solution to the marginality of low-income bike users was to increase their access to driver's licenses and public transit. Transforming the streetscape and toppling car culture's regime were not on the civil rights to-do list. And why should they be? When the current bicycle advocacy movement began in the 1970s, addressing the race and class discrimination embedded in our transportation systems was not on the agenda. Over my years of studying bicycling, especially once I became an advocate for racial inclusion within bike advocacy, I did not find a consensus view that advocates should address problems beyond fixing the street for a pleasant ride. The consensus I found was that as long as the privileged bodies of riders were protected from vehicular aggression, bikes could fit neatly into an existing social order. Race and class exclusion could remain under the radar even while advocates appropriated civil rights language to express outrage about what they perceived to be exclusion from their own streets.

Whether focused on a legal right to ride on public roads or lobbying to funnel public resources toward bicycle projects, the advocacy space that emerged from the League of American Wheelmen tradition was dominated by white, male, middle-class participants whose idea of segregation referred not to race but to mode of transportation. At the same time, my job existed because there was a multiracial network of people involved in the bike movement who wanted to see bicycle advocacy represent more of us. It was becoming clear that this would mean challenging the advocacy model that tied winning to state power, something that has never been equally accessible to us all.

In the spring of 2014, I was invited to speak at an open streets national summit in L.A. organized by another national nonprofit, the Alliance for Biking & Walking. I felt proud of the work Aaron Paley and others did to show off CicLAvia there and later wrote a report ("Unfreezing the Streets") where I explained my theory of the events. The style in D.C. was to champion one very specific policy or model, the more defined the better. Maybe I should have been claiming that the ciclovía was the silver bullet that would get everyone on bikes, like what other advocates claimed as they tried to get protected bike lanes and bike share systems written into federal transportation funding programs. But that's not what I'd been hired to do. Helping to create the human infrastructure for CicLAvia had been exciting, but it was actually the City of Lights puzzle of how to get political advocacy to reflect the concerns and values of a diverse movement that seemed like the bigger project to me now. My focus had shifted from opening streets to opening the network.

Burning Out

11

In August 2014, a nightmare came to life. I awoke to the shrill sound of my husband's phone, and the name on the screen was my sister's. Why would Gia call Ben's phone? Immediately, I knew something was wrong. I answered.

"Mom's alive," Gia's voice quavered urgently. "Mom's alive." Her tone made it sound like this was good news. I rushed through the house looking for my own phone, and saw that I'd missed several calls from her. Adrenaline surging through our veins, Gia and I went back and forth incoherently until I understood that our mother Laurene had been struck by a car in Newport Beach. She and her boyfriend were crossing the street to get back to their car after a jazz concert. The police had called Gia using Mom's phone and she bravely took on the role of point person, letting her four siblings know that our mother was alive and on her way to a local hospital.

After 24 hours of limbo, I finally made it across the country to my mother's side. She lay there in a hospital bed in Santa Ana—weak, vulnerable, incoherent from pain drugs. Her face was still bloody. Her leg was broken in four places. I would later see purple and yellow bruising all over her body when nurses helped her use a bedpan.

The man who hit Laurene and Jeff with his Mercedes Benz was driving with a suspended license. He was black. He was probably driving illegally because he didn't have other options for getting around, in this region where people commute sometimes a hundred miles a day for work and where underfunded public transit makes it difficult to travel at night without a car. He probably cared a lot about that Mercedes, a mobile status symbol, when he turned left and smashed his vehicle into two human bodies, one of which happened to have produced mine. The driver cooperated with police, and obviously felt terrible about what he had done. Even as they were loading her shocked, broken body onto the ambulance, my mom heard him saying "I'm so sorry. I'm so sorry."

My mother has been very supportive of my work with bicycling and culture change. She provided the model for it with her own cross-cultural activism in my divided hometown. As the PTA president, she had fought to keep our elementary school racially integrated and led a community task force to try and bridge between the Spanish-speaking and English-speaking residents. After the first CicLAvia, she bought a bicycle and started a train/ bike commute from her home in San Juan Capistrano to her office in Santa Ana. She wrote about it on my blog in October 2011:

> So, what have I gleaned from my week of going carfree? Principally, I have learned that human beings are very adaptable – much more so than one might generally assume. Most significantly, for me anyway, I have learned that riding the train and biking to and from the train stations is FUN. It is interesting to ride through neighborhoods instead of sitting in traffic on the freeway. I see and interact with people, both on my bike and on the train or waiting for it. When the train broke down we gathered together and communicated with each other. On the freeway when something similar happens people sit in their cars and bitch to themselves. I have time on the train to read or nap. By the time I get to work I have exercised and interacted with other human beings. Because I get to work early I have more time to get ready for my work day. I have discovered businesses along the way that I plan to frequent.

My mother is my main source of wisdom about this world and the people in it. When I was a kid, during my parents' long divorce, nothing scared me more than the thought of losing her. And now street contempt, the thing I'd become an activist to fight, threatened to take her away. None of my efforts had kept her safe.

I'd already been feeling dislocated across the continent. D.C. is a twenty-year-old smoking a cigar, a friend quipped, overrun by youth with an uncritical desire to access power, from Capitol Hill to the pockets where racialized poverty manages to keep gentrification at bay. I felt like a total outsider in the black-and-white checkerboard of neighborhoods that made up D.C. beyond expensive international zones like Dupont Circle. This was in part because I felt more and more like an outsider to the cause I had moved there to support. On paper, LAB wanted to create a racially integrated agenda. In practice, I was being treated more and more like an enemy for doing the job they'd hired me to do. I tried to push on despite the mixed messages, but in reality I was burning out.

When I agreed to manage the Equity Initiative, I had been told to expect a lot of freedom because we were breaking new ground. We hired Queta González from the Portland-based Center for Diversity and the Environment (CDE) to advise us, and she helped us plan a staff diversity training that she would facilitate at the end of March 2014. When she came to town for the final planning, she seemed to sense that I needed guidance, that I needed to be told to listen to my own internal responses. It was quite possible, Queta said, that in order to keep everything else running smoothly, I was ignoring the personal toll of the change work I had undertaken. Then something strange happened.

The Saturday morning before our training, I lay in bed enjoying the warmth of my husband sleeping beside me. My eyes trailed to a glass-paned door in the dining room, visible through the doorway.

What I saw reflected there shot me through with surprise. It was the shadow of a short, full-shouldered woman, who I knew to be Mexican. What was she doing in our apartment? I turned to my husband to alert him to the presence of this intruder, who had crept in so quietly she had escaped notice. As I touched him, I understood what I was seeing: the image of a hanging dress, reflected at an angle by the glass.

Later that day, Gia texted me. Tía Elena had died in Mexico. This great aunt, from whom I got my middle name, raised our father in their village in Nayarit. Was it her shadow I saw reflected in the glass? Why would she come to me, a distant, half-gringa, second-generation child who she never saw beyond infancy? Maybe it was the namesake. What did she want me to know, I wondered? The question followed me to the office, where I put out my hand to turn on a lamp and at the same moment I felt a jolt and the lights went out. I told Queta about all this, and she took it in stride.

The training went well, with the clumsiness and fear to be expected from a group of well-meaning white people trying to develop awareness about their privilege. But for me it ended on a disappointing note because my boss Andy had left without saying anything hours early on the second day. We had scheduled the training around his travel plans so that he could participate in the whole thing. Queta had emphasized the importance of leadership in this work, and afterwards, debriefing with Jakob and me, she brought up the disappearance with a sigh. She said that the two of us would need to stay in close communication in order to move the diversity and inclusion work forward at the organization, since we didn't have leadership buy-in.

At the board level, there was still confusion about why I was there and what I was doing. A committee had been established to help coordinate board-level education and training, but the vagueness of what we were trying to achieve overall made it difficult to organize action there. One board member had joined the Bike Equity Network email list, where she replied to a thread and reprimanded a poster for bringing up race and gender issues. To have an internal authority figure undermining my work for the organization put me in an awkward position. When multiple EAC members emailed me and demanded action, I removed the board member from the email list, but she continued on in her leadership role. Then, when a new African-American board member said she would not participate in a diversity training with white board members, the board-level work effectively got scrapped.

Over time, I figured out that a lack of a statement defining what we meant by equity, diversity, and inclusion was not about giving me freedom to innovate. It was about avoiding an uncomfortable subject. And I was in the unenviable position of being the person paid to bring it up. One confusing moment came in the summer of 2014, when it seemed like I had been too direct while others were dancing around a topic in a staff meeting. As was usually the case, I had been the only person of color in the room. Because I thought the right thing to do was to support my colleagues through their discomfort, I found myself sitting in a park with a white man who told me that I hurt his feelings when I criticized the organization. I didn't know what to say. I hadn't meant to hurt anybody's feelings, and, as Queta had noticed, I was even putting their feelings before mine. It was getting harder for me to believe that I was going to be able to change this organization's culture.

Soon after that, I left for the Latina/o Studies Association's biennial conference, where I heard a university administrator put into words the pressure I felt. "Our challenge," she said, "is to not become part of the systems we were hired to change." It was comforting to hear that my situation was typical rather than unusual. I had been hired to change an organization, and I was being confronted by how difficult it is to take an idea like that from paper to practice. It's much easier for the status quo to assimilate one person than it is for one person to change the status quo.

I had a lot of time to feel powerless when my planned vacation home in August turned into the nightmare of my mother's injury. I spent a few nights in the hospital next to her, and while she slept a drugged sleep, I watched the nightly fireworks launched from Disneyland sporadically brighten the hazy orange sky. What a war zone, I thought, where any body in the way is the enemy. We carry the threat of violence in the vehicles that take us to work, to the grocery store, to Grandma's house, on road trips, and, as I learned again that weekend, that take us to the hospital where we sit beside our people. (It is an awful trial to navigate hostile freeways to get to your loved one who lies broken after having been wounded in the street.) We direct vehicular contempt aimlessly, striking at random, flailing horsepower like peacocks' tails, and instantly become defensive when this violence is named.

Professionally, I felt like I was hitching by the side of a road while cars blew past me. I'd completely misjudged how wide the gap was between design-oriented urbanism and the movements fighting to end racism's burdens. I thought I could be a bridge across it but instead I was stuck in the middle. This was driven home in May 2014, when Carolyn and I presented on the Equity Initiative at a convening of projects funded by the same grant program. The foundation had invited a racial justice expert to speak, and we were excited to learn that he'd be our discussant. In the presentation, I did my best to explain our effort to bring the realities of marginal bike users into a policy-oriented advocacy space in order to make its agenda more equitable. But our discussant immediately made it clear that he didn't get the value of our work. I don't know if he dismissed bicycling because he associated it with white privilege or if he had some other beef with it, but in any case it wasn't encouraging.

Giving up on networking, I started looking for more people who could simply see things the way I did, especially people of color working on environmental sustainability. A great beacon was a project called Green 2.0, which released a report on "The State of Diversity in the Mainstream Environmental Sector" in 2014. They'd found that racial diversity at environmental nonprofit organizations, foundations, and government agencies was confined to the lower ranks, while leadership remained overwhelmingly white. They called for action in order to transform the environmental movement to reflect the country. I attended the press conference for the release and hoped to put together a similar analysis of the bike world. Queta's organization, CDE, had also launched a national network called Environmental Professionals of Color (EPOC), which acknowledged that we were isolated voices who needed each other's support. I joined the email list for their D.C. group. In spaces like that, I didn't need to explain that I was caught between movements.

LAB's board and leadership never gave me an answer on what defined the organization's commitment to equity. With no guidance and sensing the fear I provoked, it started to seem like my real job was to protect white men's feelings from the world I represented in my brown skin. I walked on eggshells each time I made a statement on the blog or tried to create a report. My anxiety increased with the equity toolkit, which was supposed to be the centerpiece of the grant project. Toolkits are a resource trend that sometimes offer useful advice and sometimes do little more than fulfill a grant requirement. We wanted to make ours into something that would answer the questions we had been hearing from advocates around the country who were ready to see the bike as a tool for social justice, and we recorded their stories, extrapolating advice. Carolyn and her assistant Liz Murphy helped out by interviewing a long list of our contacts who had insights into making biking more inclusive. I sourced ideas and content from the Bike Equity Network, and got great advice from LAB's new Women Bike program manager, Liz Cornish. We had sections on "real talk," anonymized stories from people who had encountered awkward moments around race with lessons learned. We had a glossary of terms that pointed toward the whole world of resources already out there defining equity, diversity, and inclusion such as the excellent Racial Equity Tools website.

I was really worried about going "too far," so I made sure to share drafts with Jakob and others in the office. I gave a presentation to all staff of the near-final draft and responded to their comments. We were planning to launch the toolkit at the upcoming Alliance for Biking & Walking's Leadership Retreat, a professional development weekend, and had also organized our own conference, Future Bike, to follow the street design convention Pro Walk Pro Bike Pro Place held in Pittsburgh in September 2014.

Despite what I thought was careful planning, my fears were realized just before we were supposed to send our final draft to the printers. Andy had concerns about the tone of the toolkit, and wanted certain sections cut out entirely. At a loss for what to do, I contacted the board equity committee and shared the draft with them, looking for advice on what action to take. For this, Andy called me into his office and demanded to know why I had dared to contact the board. Jakob stepped in on my behalf and explained that I had followed our established protocol in working with the board equity committee. Andy's distant ambivalence regarding my work had turned into what felt like a very personal dislike. I was glad to have a supervisor there to deflect some of it.

Presenting at the Leadership Retreat on my 31st birthday, without the toolkit we'd worked so hard on, we tried to make lemons into lemonade. We turned our workshop into a reflection on the friction to be expected in transforming white-centered organizations into multiracial ones. But it was hard to know where to go from there. We had the funding; we had the expertise; we didn't have buy-in from leadership. Andy's anger toward me made it seem like there was nothing I could do about that. More and more after that he treated me like an opposing force, and some colleagues followed his lead. My ethnographic investigation of human infrastructure had turned into a very uncomfortable example of me failing to fit into one. I was living the awkward truth that individual preferences can have an effect on an entire field, when the individual in question holds a position of influence.

What I went through is not unique. The frustration of a blocked chain of command, a board of directors who won't be accountable to the principles they set— I'm hardly the first nonprofit employee or woman of color to encounter these barriers. However, I don't think most people have a movement cheering them on. I was working in D.C. because some bike people appreciated my critical perspective. I wasn't just an insolent upstart in a disagreement with a seasoned boss about what my job should be; I had friends and strangers around the country telling me they believed I was on the right track. There was a long list of people I could call when I needed a pep talk. In my tiny corner of the universe, I was the Great Brown Hope. That's why I kept trying to make things work.

Even though the equity toolkit got blocked, we went on with the conference we'd planned in Pittsburgh. Future Bike was a one-day summit for people working on bike equity issues. We had "build your favorite childhood memory" workshops with my L.A. friend James Rojas, panels on various inclusion topics, and started the day by asking our 130 attendees to identify what they saw as an important but verboten topic in bicycle advocacy. They wrote these topics on sheets with an outline of an elephant and we hung them up around the hall, bringing our "elephants in the room" out into the open. At the end of the day, we asked them to write what they saw as the future we should all work towards together. Later that fall, we repurposed some of the stories from the indefinitely stalled toolkit into a separate report called "The New Movement" that profiled many of the activists out there redefining bicycling.

I saw movement building as an important component of the Equity Initiative, and yet at LAB there was nothing but resistance to plugging in these insights from the grassroots bike movement. For example, any of my contacts' testimonials about the power of community-led planning processes seemed like they should have been enough to make the shortcomings of the top-down infrastructure approach obvious. But that approach was not up for debate. While I had understood that street infrastructure was a trend that had been circulating among bike advocates since the 1990s, I did not anticipate how invested in it the national bike lobby would be. Now that I was in D.C., I could see that bike organizations were there to create demand for the bike industry, and today's bike industry included a plethora of planning and design firms that lived off government contracts to write and implement bike plans.

This was not nefarious in itself; many advocates are in D.C. to try and direct public funding toward some industry or other. But it did mean that the infrastructure strategy was there to stay, to the degree that I'm not sure my colleagues ever really listened to what alternatives I had in mind. Securing funding and getting design standards adopted for street infrastructure were *the* end goals of advocacy, not means to some other end. It seemed that what was allowable equity-wise was to brand infrastructure as desperately needed in low-income neighborhoods. To me this seemed to be a far cry from meaningful participation, just churning out more spokespeople for predetermined goals rather than bringing them into movement leadership and potentially changing those goals. I wanted to do something more transformative than use people of color as a front, but the leadership at LAB wasn't interested in adding to their agenda unless new ideas came from a very specific network of peer organizations, mostly based in New York,

San Francisco, Portland, and Chicago. Again, there was nothing inherently unethical about this; vetting ideas through networks is how human infrastructure operates. However, given the history of bicycle racism and the white advocacy space it produced, maintaining a closed network in effect meant that ideas from individuals who didn't fit in with that network didn't find support.

I saw just how closed the network could be in the aftermath of the vehicular cycling debate, when the leadership at LAB simply cut ties with some of its LCIs and advocates. Disagreement was expected to be vicious and irreparable. This was the polar opposite of the expanding, blending, human infrastructure approach I'd brought with me. I was working on bicycling because I loved being part of the bike movement, with its eccentrics, its enthusiastic women of color starting bike media and design businesses, its impassioned parents fighting to make it okay for their kids to ride bikes in the street, its anarchist punks training fourteen year olds how to wrench, its friendly men of color who join community rides on their tricked-out cruisers, its clueless-about-social-justice-but-willing-to-learn older white men. To me, opening the network meant finding our common ground. It was becoming clearer that this rapprochement was not the vision dominant at LAB.

I needed help dealing with these professional setbacks, so I found a therapist. When she asked me to visualize a place where I felt calm, I knew just where to look. When I was 14 and isolated from my peers by family sorrow, my mother decided to take my little sister and me on a road trip to Sedona, Arizona. We visited a AAA office, gathered maps, and had fun tracing our route along the many lines of interstate between our home in San Juan and our destination in the desert. On the morning of the first day, we crossed over the Santa Ana Mountains and I saw the blue pitches of desert and further ranges beyond them. It felt good to leave a hard year behind.

Hiking over the red rocks of high-desert Arizona, I made up a game to occupy my mind. I was a scout for a tribe, a young man who knew every sound and shadow in these valleys. He stood among the piñons on light feet, watching the strange interlopers on the hiking trail below. Who were these newcomers, he wondered, and what did they presage for his people? He existed in a moment before the cascading death and change that we refer to blandly as "contact," and in that moment, he knew more about that landscape than anyone else. Nobody could surprise him there. They would eventually overwhelm his social order by brute force, not by a greater local knowledge.

I played the game for years when hiking. I never said much about it, but as my body lay in the attic room of a counseling center in Northeast D.C. and I heard the dry wind in a high desert canyon, it occurred to me that my blood is mixed. My older sister's genealogical research has shown that I likely got about a quarter of my DNA from an indigenous group in Mexico. Among my five siblings, my body phenotypically shows our Indigenous heritage most strongly.

The next morning, steeling myself for another day of anxiety-filled meetings where I would have to defend my right to see the world from my own coordinates, I got an odd sense of distance as I stood looking through the successive doorways echoing down the narrow hall of my railroad flat. All the way back, across five hundred years, a thread stretched. And it connected me to the scout—it was a lineage beyond doubt. All the artillery, all the disease, all the effects of internalized shame, could only make us mixed-up selves. In me, in us, something despised survived, despite the deliberate attempt to stamp out particular contributors to our DNA. I am a product of the truth that racial contempt has never been as stubborn as life.

The wall I'd hit at work felt too much like the street contempt I'd gotten into this movement to fight. My boss didn't trust me enough to tell me why he reacted to me the way he did, but I wondered if it had to with me being a brown woman whose earlier success with projects like CicLAvia made me pretty confident that I had some good advocacy ideas. My new co-worker, Liz Cornish, hit the same wall, and she was a white woman also accustomed to playing a leadership role in bicycling. We'd both been hired because the advocacy network was too inbred to survive, but perhaps it was inevitable that my difference pushed me out before I could change it.

I saw how truly limited in scope my contribution was expected to be when our boss informed us that a new safety program, Vision Zero, would now be the thread that connected all our work and our jobs would be to incorporate it into our program areas. This raised red flags for me. My work there was supposed to be creating the infrastructure so that new ideas and people could be part of the bike advocacy establishment. Instead, I was being asked to equity-wash this new silver bullet that fit the same old mold: Northern European origins, pushed through via political capital rather than grassroots organizing, emergent from within the closed network of advocacy organizations.

In the fall of 2014, I was sent to a Vision Zero conference in New York, and saw more red flags in their emphasis on police enforcement of traffic laws. I knew from L.A. how uninterested in feedback police departments can be, and how they protected individual officers' discretion, so I was unconvinced that Vision Zero supporters actually had the ability to direct police priorities. More than that, traffic stops are a common starting point for what ends in state-sanctioned violence against black and brown bodies. The timing for Vision Zero seemed way off given the hard work people were putting into building popular support for police reform. This was right when the Black Lives Matter movement had made racialized police violence into national news. The women who founded BLM pointed to the treatment of black people's bodies, very specifically. Bike advocates were again looking to a state resource as a trusted ally and overlooking the racism that subjected certain groups to less safety. When I raised these concerns in a meeting at work, Andy told the room that it wasn't my business to have opinions about it.

Near the end of 2014, I made another attempt to salvage the Equity Initiative, asking Andy to draw a map of how all of LAB's programs fit together. Then we could work as a team—he, Jakob, and I—to define actions that enhanced each of these programs. I thought if I could get him to decide what my work should be, he'd feel less threatened by my presence. He seemed enthusiastic, but then never produced what I'd asked for.

And then suddenly Jakob was gone. From the frightening meeting I sat through with Andy soon after, it seemed like Jakob had committed what I'd already learned was a sin in Andy's eyes: he'd communicated with the board. In that meeting, Andy told me that if I wanted to keep my job, I would need to remain loyal to him. "I'm here to support this organization's mission," I replied carefully, trying to conceal how fast my heart was beating. I was baffled that he expected me to respond to his obvious animosity toward me with some oath of allegiance, as though I'd been a conspirator trying to undermine his power and needed to repent. Without Jakob there to give me cover, I felt more unwelcome than ever and started working mostly from home. It was small comfort to know that I wasn't alone in this unpleasant atmosphere; there was a group of other women who were also being treated like a threat.

I had never fully shaken the anxiety that would rise in my chest when I spoke publicly about the intersections of race and bicycling, and after fifteen months of being treated like something to be feared rather than a trusted colleague, I lost my bearings and spiraled into uncertainty. Maybe my attempts to advocate for the realities of people of color and low-income bike users *were* dangerous; maybe I *could* say the wrong words and the world would tumble down. I don't know if anybody did this to me out of malice or spite, or with any intention at all. It can be confusing to be a woman of color.

I took a trip to Seattle in February 2015 for the Youth Bike Summit, the most multicultural and multiracial bike event out there at the time. As a keynote speaker in front of a theater full of young people, I thought about how I didn't want them to go through the confusion I was living. From my work at LAB, I'd deduced that the folks who saw themselves as calling the shots in bicycle advocacy viewed people of color like me and most of the kids in the audience as tokens. We were free to build a movement they could use to show popular support for their agenda when convenient. We were not to disrupt the years of networking and planning white advocates had done to promote the bicycle gentrification strategy. I told the audience to stick with their values and to pay attention to moments when they felt asked to leave those values aside.

Before I left for Seattle, I'd drafted a letter to the LAB board laying out what I saw as the barriers to me performing my job tasks and meeting grant deliverables, and I asked that they intervene. When I got back to D.C., the board chair called me and told me they would be taking no action, so I let him know I quit. Suddenly I felt lighter than I had in a long, long time.

An Other Kind of Power

After burning out at LAB, I kind of just wanted to be done with bike advocacy. It was going to be controversial for me to state what was true for so many people as long as advocates preferred to view issues like racism as utterly separate from bicycle planning and policy. What was the point of probing bicycling's intersections if this information didn't matter to those who felt entitled to speak for all bicycle users? Beyond feeling like my research was going nowhere, I also felt tokenized. Hiring me meant that LAB could make public claims about equity, diversity, and inclusion, while avoiding systemic change. All I had done was parade my difference, over and over, telling the public that within this organization they were making room for people like me. The toll this tokenism took on me? In a word: *Stresssssssssss.*

Many people of color have been recruited to do tokenizing work; I knew from my conversations with others in bicycle advocacy and similar fields that it wasn't just me. I'd started attending a peer therapy group for people of color working at predominantly white environmental organizations. In that space, I heard others talk about being careful with their words and behavior at work, like I had been. Clearly I wasn't alone in feeling like I saw the world differently than my colleagues did and that they didn't want to hear about it. So why had it felt so personal?

A few months after leaving my job at LAB, as I was telling my sister Gia about my confusion, she went and found a book on her shelf. It was *Emplumada*, a book of poetry by Lorna Dee Cervantes. Before the poems began, there was an epigram: "Consider the power of wrestling your ally. His will is to kill you. He has nothing against you." This conundrum perfectly described the reality I was inhabiting, and with this quotation, my sister told me that it is a reality that many women like me inhabit. Crossing boundaries is normal for us, but others see our shape shifting as a threat. We feel the sting of poison and are called enemies by people who never have to look in the mirror and see their own faces twisted with hate.

Maybe a big reason why I hadn't fit in at LAB was that I never learned to act like a white man's daughter. My mother never learned, because her father was so cartoonishly unkind that she saw him for the selfish tyrant he was. My grandmother didn't learn, because her father died when she was five. My mother's whiteness protected me in this racist world and gave me the freedom to love myself, because she loved me, her mother loved me, her grandmother loved me. I thought I could succeed being my mixed self in white spaces because my family intervened to make me proud, not self-loathing. I've had the freedom to be more concerned about the dark shoulders supporting me than about reaching white hands that might reluctantly lift *just me* up from the collective.

Since I grew up with women, I had to learn later that the world tells men (and especially white men) that their feelings were my fault. I learned to fear their anger, and I'd turned on myself, becoming uneasy narrating the world as I saw it. My fears blurred together. Fear of ecological disaster, fear that when I shared my insights I'd hear a chorus of boos, fear of the look of anger I'd seen in my boss' eyes at LAB. How far back did this fear go? Hadn't it been a familiar feeling even when I was getting started with my project back in 2008? I started meeting regularly with a bodywork therapist who helped me to pinpoint and release the fear that had taken me over. I got to know what it felt like to go days without my adrenaline spiking. When I interfaced with bike advocacy, I tried to witness how anxious I felt about calling out unexamined racism. It wasn't just bike advocacy, either; white people were speaking for the future of our cities in many issue areas.

Feeling out of touch with my white side and outside of urbanism, I imagined life in a pre-colonial era. Before the imposition of European norms on everyone in the Americas, there were other systems and aesthetics, ways of expressing human creativity and emotion. I could not say whether these social orders were better or worse than what I've known, but they ran along different lines. In the D.C. heat, I was drawn to the cool halls of Smithsonian museums, and I sought out exhibits about past worlds forever changed by colonialism's contempt. I went to George Catlin's paintings of Native men and women hanging in a stairwell at the National Portrait Gallery. There were similar paintings in an exhibition on broken treaties at the National Museum of the American Indian. The subjects were confident and peacocking figures clad in colorful bits and pieces, their own trophies. They gazed out at the viewer with something less interested than defiance.

I read the conquistador Bernal Diaz del Castillo's account of the Spanish expedition into Mexico and found it fascinating as he recounted visiting cities so alien to his eyes that he struggled to describe them. I tried to imagine floating past Tenochtitlan's agricultural islands called chinampas and smelling the blood of sacrifice. Not necessarily better or worse, but on other terms. Of course, the conquerors were not there to be anthropologists–to patiently wait and live and breathe and over time watch a logic emerge. What survived was what colonizers didn't think was even worth destroying. They slashed and they burned and they scarred us into mestizaje. And here I am. Yet somehow these centuries of racial intermingling have not been enough on their own to stop the illusion of division, at least in my part of North America.

Riding the train down the west coast, I've seen long stretches of abandoned infrastructure. These are the remnants of old telegraph systems and signal lines for the railroads, and many of the functions this infrastructure used to serve have been replaced by other technologies. Between the poles lie downed strings of wire, tangled messes. Glass and porcelain insulators are jumbled about, blue and green and clear slugs that you can buy in antique stores. I don't think much information flows through this system anymore, but we're letting it stay up until it falls down.

It occurred to me that racism is similar. The human infrastructure of racism trained people to keep separate, with reprimands big and little sent down the line to those who deviated. Over time, the moral project of segregation didn't need to be enforced anymore because we lived divided out of habit. Blatantly racist Grandpa became a cause for rolled eyes at Thanksgiving, a relic of a shameful past. Nobody explained that his generation's racism primed Mom and Dad to avoid raising their children around people of color, using rationalizations like "good schools."

It's been passed down to us. When I took a bike advocacy job at the national level, I thought I was joining a collaborative effort to dismantle a decommissioned racial hierarchy. I thought I was there to put my brand new PhD. to work for a shared cause. Instead, I started receiving harsher messages than I'd heard since I was a brown kid in a white paradise. The lines put in place to maintain racism maybe don't crackle for white people like they used to, but people of color can see that the structures still stand in the hearts and minds of those who fear us.

I believe that our relationships can transform this outdated system. The fact is that I would not still be talking or writing about bicycling if it wasn't for the other thinkers and activists who surround me. I would have jumped ship, like I wanted to after leaving LAB, like other brilliant activists I know who moved on to other movements because they felt so unwelcome in bicycling. My social entanglement in this work holds me accountable. So I started to wonder, how do I fit into the system that upholds inequity along racial lines?

I thought of a San Juan Capistrano story that they hadn't told us in school. In 1889, a woman named Modesta Avila secured a wooden post across the new tracks that the Santa Fe Railroad had put down next to her family's house on Calle Los Rios. To this post she attached a sign informing the railroad interests that they would need to pay for the use of her land if they wanted to run trains over it. Modesta was born to a mestizo family in San Juan in 1867. Historian Lisbeth Haas has found that by the time of her protest, Modesta's family had already lost legal title to the plot they lived on, due to the land grab where U.S. settlers dispossessed Mexican and Indigenous families through debt, taxes, and long legal battles.[45]

Even though she didn't have a legal right to her family's land under the U.S. regime, maybe Modesta thought that her act of resistance would find support among fellow remnants of Mexican California, that she'd be a celebrated outlaw like Joaquin Murrieta or Tiburcio Vasquez. The law rebuked Modesta strongly for claiming that she should have some say in what was happening

---

45 Haas provides the details of Avila's case in her great essay on California women's assertion of property rights (citation in note 14). Haas called Modesta's attempt to tap into the economic growth spurred by the railroad, and to be compensated for the hazard traveling feet from where her family slept, a "protest against the new order."

right next to her home, and nobody came to her rescue. For her obstruction of the railroad, Orange County's courthouse in Santa Ana sentenced Avila, the brand new county's first felon, to three years in San Quentin Prison. She died there before the end of her sentence.

The injustice of Modesta's imprisonment and death stung me when I learned of it in college. I was born right next to those railroad tracks she died for defying, a few hundred yards away from the site of her protest. The tracks penned us in against the hills full of coyotes who yipped in rounds when the late night trains rumbled into the valley. Now, as I started probing my own entanglement in the colonial system, I thought about how I was born there right next to those tracks because train tracks like the ones in which Modesta was denied an equity share carried millions of settlers into Southern California. The emotional bonds of family have tied us to the region since the 1890s, so I never felt like a settler. And yet it's all there in the historical record, my great-greats who developed buildings, speculated on rural land, and acquired acreage for agriculture. Their European heritage gave them legal cover to harvest the fruits of this place where they had just arrived.

For many of us who benefited from those old colonial land grabs, those conquests have been followed by our own loss. Take my grandma's house, for example. The coastal bluff where Grandma and Great Grandma's house in Corona Del Mar sat is in the ancestral territory of the Acjachemen people. It began its life as an exchangeable good when it was claimed by the faraway king of Spain. Then, through a Mexican land grant, it became part of Rancho San Joaquin, owned by the Californio José Sepulveda. After a devastating drought, he sold it in 1864 to the Irish immigrant whose descendants founded the Irvine Company, which is still a dominant force in Orange County development today. The property may have passed through the hands of several other subdividers before my great grandma's second husband bought it and built the cottage for our family at 321 Marigold in the 1940s.

Before the matriarchs passed away and the house was sold, it had been the site of all our holiday gatherings and birthdays. I loved clambering over the same rocks at the beach that my mom and her siblings had claimed as thrones back when they were little. I played under the shade of the avocado tree next to the wishing well built by the step-great-grandfather who died long before I was born. It was my sanctuary.

We grumbled about how the house went for about $500,000 in the late 1990s, less than others in the neighborhood because it was a buyer's market. Within a decade, the house had been flipped and re-flipped for twice that selling price. We all still visited the house from time to time, showing it to the people important to us. We would park outside Grandma's house and walk the two blocks to Main Beach or Pirate's Cove like we always had. That's how we learned it was gone, when one day my cousin drove by to show the house to a friend. My sister visited the demolition site and took home some of the bricks that had either come from the house or had outlined Great Grandma's garden. I was very sad to lose the family home, but I also got a cut of the profits.

As I grappled with my place in the systems of power and privilege I wanted to change, I went to breathe in the redwoods at the home of a dear friend who worked for the UC Santa Cruz (UCSC) library, and she told me that any visitor there could request to view the collection of Gloria Anzaldúa's *altares* (altars). Anzaldúa's words had been a great comfort to me through this time period. I remember sitting at the Martin Luther King, Jr. library in D.C., reading her co-edited book *This Bridge Called My Back* and realizing that human infrastructure was not a new idea.

Since before I was born, women of color had been writing about being emotional connective tissue and bleeding when imposed boundaries sliced up their lives. It's still frowned upon for women like me to cry out when we're stepped on. We sound like whiners, like people who didn't work hard enough and don't deserve success. We tell our stories through a thick layer of stereotypes and outsiders' assumptions about what is our fault and what is our burden. Like many others before me, I found deeply familiar truths within Anzaldúa's own masterpiece, *Borderlands/La Frontera*, and I marveled at her craft and courage in baring her pain and joy.

The altares collection was available because one of the many people tied to the beloved Anzaldúa, who passed in 2004, was an oral historian at the UCSC library. She had honored her friend by making special boxes to display the hundreds of tiny figurines, souvenirs, joke gifts, that Anzaldúa would arrange in groups around her home.[46] I thought they were there for me to see, not touch, but their guardian told me to pick them up. This open gesture surprised me. The objects held power for Anzaldúa, I had read; why should I get to touch them and let that power flow into my strange hands?

There is a power that encompasses us within outwardly expanding circles of warmth. It's different than the power that tries to conserve itself by shutting most of us out in the cold. When I feel the love of that other power around me, I feel strong enough to send this message to those who see me as some kind of threat: I know you, enemy. I am your daughter's child, and when you cut me, she bleeds. I won't carry your fear inside me anymore, and I wish you would let it go.

---

46 The University of Texas at Austin took Anzaldúa's papers but not the altares. Irene, the oral historian I met, thought they should be preserved, and she was the one instrumental in bringing them to the UCSC archive.

Whether they meant to or not, bike advocates took on racial inclusion when they decided to go after public resources, because lobbying for street change doesn't take place in a vacuum separate from the legacy and reality of inequality that so many people try and fight through justice movements. Race and mobility are intertwined because we designed segregation into our built environments and how we police them, and racial equity in the distribution of public money isn't a metaphor or a goal you opt into; it's a legal obligation, thanks to the civil rights movement. I wasn't pointing to the culture of white supremacy embedded in bike advocacy, policy, and planning because I wanted to cause trouble; it was about fulfilling the promise of our shared democracy.

Unlike Modesta Avila, I'm not a one-woman rebellion. I've joined and expanded a movement toward sustainable and equitable transportation, and I'm lucky that there are other writers chronicling this work. D.C. wasn't a place where I knew how to stay connected to the other kind of power, and I didn't feel strong enough to be a center of it on my own. So I moved back to the borderlands of Southern California. I started over in active transportation with a new focus on moving the field past tokenism like what I'd gone through. But I didn't really start over, because this time I'm part of a network that stretches all over the country, one that has been growing for years.

SUBSCRIBE TO EVERYTHING WE PUBLISH!

Do you love what Microcosm publishes?

Do you want us to publish more great stuff?

Would you like to receive each new title as it's published?

Subscribe as a BFF to our new titles and we'll mail them all to you as they are released!

$10-30/mo, pay what you can afford. Include your t-shirt size and month/date of birthday for a possible surprise! Subscription begins the month after it is purchased.

microcosmpublishing.com/bff

...AND HELP US GROW YOUR SMALL WORLD!

More about bicycle culture and transportation: